CHINA (INCLUDES TIBET, HONG KONG, AND MACAU) 2016 HUMAN RIGHTS REPORT

EXECUTIVE SUMMARY

The People's Republic of China (PRC) is an authoritarian state in which the Chinese Communist Party (CCP) is the paramount authority. CCP members hold almost all top government and security apparatus positions. Ultimate authority rests with the CCP Central Committee's 25-member Political Bureau (Politburo) and its seven-member Standing Committee. Xi Jinping continued to hold the three most powerful positions as CCP general secretary, state president, and chairman of the Central Military Commission.

Civilian authorities maintained control of the military and internal security forces.

Repression and coercion of organizations and individuals involved in civil and political rights advocacy as well as in public interest and ethnic minority issues remained severe. As in previous years, citizens did not have the right to choose their government and elections were restricted to the lowest local levels of governance. Authorities prevented independent candidates from running in those elections, such as delegates to local people's congresses. Citizens had limited forms of redress against official abuse. Other serious human rights abuses included arbitrary or unlawful deprivation of life, executions without due process, illegal detentions at unofficial holding facilities known as "black jails," torture and coerced confessions of prisoners, and detention and harassment of journalists, lawyers, writers, bloggers, dissidents, petitioners, and others whose actions the authorities deemed unacceptable. There was also a lack of due process in judicial proceedings, political control of courts and judges, closed trials, the use of administrative detention, failure to protect refugees and asylum seekers, extrajudicial disappearances of citizens, restrictions on nongovernmental organizations (NGOs), discrimination against women, minorities, and persons with disabilities. The government imposed a coercive birth-limitation policy that, despite lifting one-child-per-family restrictions, denied women the right to decide the number of their children and in some cases resulted in forced abortions (sometimes at advanced stages of pregnancy). Severe labor restrictions continued, and trafficking in persons was a problem.

Although most of the more than 300 lawyers and human rights activists detained in 2015 were released, 16 remained in pretrial detention without access to attorneys or family members at year's end. Four others were sentenced to jail terms ranging from three years to seven and one-half years in trials that foreign governments and international human rights organizations said lacked basic due process. Wang Yu, one of the most prominent lawyers detained during the crackdown, was released after her televised confession, which circumstances suggest was likely coerced. Many others remained under various restrictions, including continuous residential surveillance at undisclosed locations. Public security officials continued to harass, intimidate, and take punitive measures against the family members of rights defenders and lawyers in retaliation for their work.

A new Law on the Management of Foreign NGO Activities inside Mainland China placed foreign NGOs under the supervision of the Ministry of Public Security, a move that indicated foreign NGOs were considered a "national security" threat. Although the law was not scheduled to go into effect until January 1, 2017, many foreign NGOs and their domestic partners began to curtail operations before the year's end, citing concerns over the law's vaguely worded provisions. As a result, an already limited space for civil society was further constrained. Individuals and groups regarded as politically sensitive by authorities faced tight restrictions on their freedom to assemble, practice religion, and travel both within China and overseas. Authorities used extralegal measures, such as enforced disappearances and strict house arrest, to prevent public expression of critical opinions. Authorities continued to censor and tightly control public discourse on the internet, and in print and other media. There was at least one widely reported extraterritorial disappearance that occurred during the year.

Official repression of the freedoms of speech, religion, movement, association, and assembly of Tibetans in the Tibet Autonomous Region (TAR) and other Tibetan areas and of Uighurs in the Xinjiang Uighur Autonomous Region (XUAR) continued and were more severe than in other areas of the country. In the XUAR officials sometimes subjected individuals engaged in peaceful expression of political and religious views to arbitrary arrest, harassment, and expedited judicial procedures without due process in the name of combatting terrorism.

Authorities prosecuted a number of abuses of power through the court system, particularly with regard to corruption, but in most cases the CCP first investigated and punished officials using opaque internal party disciplinary procedures. The CCP continued to dominate the judiciary and controlled the appointment of all judges and in certain cases directly dictated the court's ruling. Authorities targeted citizens who promoted independent efforts to combat abuses of power.

Section 1. Respect for the Integrity of the Person, Including Freedom from:

a. Arbitrary Deprivation of Life and other Unlawful or Politically Motivated Killings

Security forces reportedly committed arbitrary or unlawful killings. In many instances, few or no details were available.

In May environmentalist Lei Yang died under mysterious circumstances while in custody in Beijing following a brief altercation with public security officials. Authorities initially claimed 29-year-old Lei had suffered a heart attack, although an autopsy determined the cause of death was suffocation. Lei's body also showed bruising on his arms and head. A subsequent investigation found that public security officials had blocked the inquiry into the cause of Lei's death. In June, two public security officers were arrested on suspicion of "dereliction of duty." Subsequent reporting on the case was censored. In late December officials announced that five law enforcement officers would not stand trial for Lei's death.

In December, 58-year-old democracy activist Peng Ming died under suspicious circumstances in prison. His family was unable to view the body, and authorities denied his adult children permission to enter the country to collect his ashes.

In June, Tibetan Buddhist nun Yeshi Lhakdron of Kardze prefecture in the Tibetan area of Kham, now administered under Sichuan Province, died in custody due to torture, according to the Tibetan Center for Human Rights. Also in June a 40-year-old man from Kardze who was detained on suspicion of possessing a gun died in custody, reportedly due to severe torture (see the Tibet Annex for further information).

Authorities did not account for the circumstances surrounding the 2015 death of Zhang Liumao, who died suddenly in custody in Guangzhou after being detained and charged with "picking quarrels and provoking trouble." His family's lawyer found his corpse was bruised with apparent signs of torture. He had not yet been tried at the time of his death. During the year Zhang's sister, Zhang Wuzhou, made multiple attempts to file lawsuits against the government over the mishandling of her brother's forensic report. Public security imposed a foreign travel ban on her and detained her outside a Guangzhou courthouse in April. The court eventually accepted the lawsuit.

A number of violent incidents in the XUAR resulted in multiple deaths. For example, media reported that at least five persons, including two public security officers, died in May as a result of violent unrest sparked when an officer allegedly shot and killed a Uighur prisoner in a juvenile detention center in Urumqi. Official accounts of these events generally blamed "terrorists" or "separatists" and portrayed incidents involving violence as terrorist attacks on community members and security personnel. The government's control of information coming out of the XUAR, together with its increasingly tight security posture there, made it difficult to verify reports (see also the Tibet annex for incidents of abuse).

Although legal reforms in recent years decreased the use of the death penalty and improved the review process, authorities executed some defendants in criminal proceedings following convictions that lacked due process and adequate channels for appeal.

b. Disappearance

There were multiple reports of individuals detained by authorities and held at undisclosed locations.

As of the end of the year, 16 individuals detained as a result of the July 2015 "709" roundup of more than 300 human rights lawyers and legal associates remained in pretrial detention at undisclosed locations without access to attorneys or to their family members. The crackdown primarily targeted those individuals who worked as defense lawyers on prominent human rights and public interest cases, including the 2008 melamine scandal, the Beijing "feminist five" detentions, the Xu Chunhe case, and cases involving the sexual abuse of young girls. The clients of those targeted included jailed Uighur economist Ilham Tohti, members of unregistered churches, and Falun Gong practitioners. The names of those who were still detained at the end of the year are Li Heping, Xie Yanyi, Wang Quanzhang, Liu Sixin, Xie Yang, Li Chunfu, Wu Gan, Lin Bin, Yin Xu'an, Wang Fang, Zhang Wanhe, Liu Xing, Li Yanjun, Yao Jianqing, Tang Zhishun, and Xing Qianxian.

Jiang Tianyong, a lawyer who advocated on behalf of the family members of the "709" detainees, disappeared on November 21 in Henan Province. He subsequently was placed under "residential surveillance at an undisclosed location" on suspicion of "inciting subversion of state power."

While several "709" detainees still awaited trial, some lawyers were convicted in trials lacking due process (see section 1.e.), and others were released on bail from formal custody after detentions that lasted, in many cases, more than a year. For example, in August attorney Wang Yu was released from detention after the government released a video that many observers called a forced confession. In the video Wang said she would no longer allow herself to be "used by foreign forces." Wang's attorney learned about her release when he saw the televised statement. Wang's husband, law associate Bao Longjun, was released as well in August. The couple was reportedly reunited with their son, Bao Zhuoxuan, who had tried to flee the country via Burma in 2015, where he was intercepted by government agents and returned to China. The couple's lawyer and other friends and associates were unable to contact them since their release from formal detention, and reports indicated that they remained under some form of residential surveillance and detention.

In March lawyer Zhang Kai was released from detention after seven months. Zhang was known for his work defending Wenzhou Christian churches that faced demolition or forced cross removals. He had been detained in 2015 on the eve of a planned meeting with a prominent foreign diplomat. Zhang's release also followed a statement in which he "confessed " on state-run television to his alleged crimes and urged other citizens "not to collude with foreigners." In August, Zhang took to social media to recant his earlier confession, which he said was made under conditions of duress. Authorities responded by surrounding his family home and threatening to rearrest him. Zhang remained under house arrest and was not able to resume his legal duties.

A number of extraterritorial disappearances occurred during the year. Former *Southern Metropolis Daily* journalist Li Xin, who fled to India in 2015 after allegedly leaking documents detailing the Communist Party's propaganda policies, went missing on a train in Thailand in January and later reappeared in China in custody of security officials. He told his wife by telephone that he had returned voluntarily, but Thai immigration officials told the media they had no exit record for Li.

Five men working in Hong Kong's publishing industry disappeared between October and December 2015. In addition to being Hong Kong residents, Gui Minhai was a Swedish citizen and was taken while he was in Thailand; Lee Bo was a British citizen taken from Hong Kong. Media coverage of the cases noted that the men worked for Mighty Current, a publishing house, and its affiliate, Causeway Bay Bookstore, which were known for selling books critical of the CCP and its leaders. In a televised "confession" released by Chinese authorities in the spring, Gui Minhai said he had "voluntarily returned" to China to "bear the responsibility" for a traffic accident that supposedly occurred more than a decade before. Another bookseller, Hong Kong resident Lam Wing Kee, was detained at the border crossing into Shenzhen in October 2015 and released after five months. Upon his return to Hong Kong, Lam immediately recanted his televised confession, saying it was scripted and recorded under extreme pressure. He also said he was forced to sign away his legal rights when he was taken to Ningbo by men who claimed they were from a "central special unit." With the exception of Swedish citizen Gui Minhai, the other detained booksellers were released during the year but remained under surveillance, travel restrictions, and the threat of punishment after returning to Hong Kong. At year's end Gui remained in incommunicado detention in the mainland.

The government still had not provided a comprehensive, credible accounting of all those killed, missing, or detained in connection with the violent suppression of the 1989 Tiananmen demonstrations. The Dui Hua Foundation reported that Miao Deshun, the last known political prisoner dating from the Tiananmen era, was released during the year. Many activists who were involved in the 1989 demonstrations and their family members continued to suffer official harassment. Chen Yunfei, arrested in 2015 for visiting the grave of a Tiananmen victim, was formally brought to trial in July on charges of "picking quarrels and provoking troubles." Chengdu authorities subsequently postponed his trial without explanation. In December a rescheduled hearing was also reportedly delayed after Chen dismissed his lawyers, citing their harassment at the hands of local security officials outside the courthouse. Others who attempted to commemorate the protests and associated deaths were themselves detained or otherwise targeted. In late May, seven activists who appeared in a photograph marking the massacre's 27th anniversary were detained on suspicion of "picking quarrels and provoking troubles." They were released several weeks later. In June, Chengdu activists Fu Hailu, Zhang Junyong, Luo Yufu, and Chen Bing were detained for allegedly creating and marketing a liquor whose label commemorated the 1989 crackdown. They faced charges of "inciting subversion" and were held in the Chengdu Municipal Detention Center.

c. Torture and Other Cruel, Inhuman, or Degrading Treatment or Punishment

The law prohibits the physical abuse and mistreatment of detainees and forbids prison guards from coercing confessions, insulting prisoners' dignity, and beating or encouraging others to beat prisoners. Amendments to the criminal procedure law exclude evidence, including coerced confessions obtained through illegal means, in certain categories of criminal cases. Enforcement of these legal protections continued to be lax.

Numerous former prisoners and detainees reported they were beaten, subjected to electric shock, forced to sit on stools for hours on end, hung by the wrists, raped, deprived of sleep, force-fed, and otherwise subjected to physical and psychological abuse. Although ordinary prisoners were abused, prison authorities reportedly singled out political and religious dissidents for particularly harsh treatment. In some instances close relatives of dissidents also were singled out for abuse.

The problem of torture was systemic, according to a UN Committee against Torture report released in December 2015 that detailed the extent to which torture was embedded in the criminal justice system. While the UN committee acknowledged some improvements, such as the broader use of surveillance cameras during interrogations, the report stated that torture was "entrenched."

A May 2015 Human Rights Watch report found continued widespread use of degrading treatment and torture by law enforcement authorities. Some courts continued to admit coerced confessions as evidence, despite the criminal procedure law, which restricts the use of unlawfully obtained evidence. After examining 158,000 criminal court verdicts published on the Supreme People's Court website, Human Rights Watch found that judges excluded confessions in only 6 percent of the cases in which torture was alleged and that all the defendants were convicted, even in the cases when evidence such was excluded. Lawyers reported that interrogators turned to less-detectable methods of torture. Confessions were often videotaped; harsh treatment beforehand was not. Lawyers who attempted to shed light on the problem of torture in the criminal justice system themselves became targets of intimidation and harassment.

Family members asserted that rights lawyer Xie Yang was repeatedly tied up and beaten during his lengthy detention in Changsha, Hunan Province. According to reports leaked from the detention facility, at one point Xie required hospitalization after he was beaten until he lost consciousness. As of December he was still in detention. There were multiple reports that other lawyers, law associates, and activists detained in the "709" crackdown also suffered various forms of torture, abuse, or degrading treatment, including Sui Muqing, whom public security officers reportedly kept awake for days on end, and Yin Xu'an, whom security agents repeatedly tortured in an attempt to extract a confession. The lawyers of Wu Gan, another "709" detainee, also reported that Wu had been tortured following their meeting with him at the Tianjin No. 2 Detention Center. Guangdong attorney Sui Muqing, who was detained in July 2015 and held under residential surveillance at an undisclosed location until the end of the year, was reportedly tortured while in custody.

Members of the minority Uighur ethnic group reported systematic torture and other degrading treatment by law enforcement officers and the penal system (see section 6, National/Racial/Ethnic Minorities). Practitioners of the banned Falun Gong spiritual movement reported systematic torture more often than other groups.

The law states that psychiatric treatment and hospitalization should be "on a voluntary basis," but it has loopholes that allow authorities and family members to commit persons to psychiatric facilities against their will and fails to provide meaningful legal protections for persons sent to psychiatric facilities. The law does not provide for the right to a lawyer and restricts a person's right to communicate with those outside the psychiatric institutions.

According to the *Legal Daily* (a state-owned newspaper covering legal affairs), the Ministry of Public Security directly administered 23 high-security psychiatric hospitals for the criminally insane (also known as ankang facilities). While many of those committed to mental health facilities had been convicted of murder and other violent crimes, there were also reports of activists and petitioners involuntarily subjected to psychiatric treatment for political reasons. Public security officials may commit individuals to ankang facilities and force treatment for "conditions" that have no basis in psychiatry. In February, one domestic NGO reported that it had tracked more than 30 cases of activists "who were forcibly committed to psychiatric institutions in 2015, often without their relatives' knowledge or consent." For example, Shanghai authorities dispatched agents to intercept petitioner Lu Liming when he was en route to Beijing to protest. They detained him in a psychiatric facility, tied him to a bed for days, beat him, and forcibly medicated him.

As of January 2015, the government claimed it was ending the long-standing practice of involuntarily harvesting the organs of executed prisoners for use in transplants. In August the official Xinhua News Agency reported 10,057 organ transplants from voluntary donors were performed in the country in 2015, with transplants expected to increase 40 to 50 percent in 2016. Some international medical professionals and human rights researchers questioned the voluntary nature of the system, the accuracy of official statistics, and official claims about the source of organs. The country has no tradition of organ donorship, and its organ donor system remained fledgling.

Prison and Detention Center Conditions

Conditions in penal institutions for both political prisoners and criminal offenders were generally harsh and often degrading.

<u>Physical Conditions</u>: Authorities regularly held prisoners and detainees in overcrowded conditions with poor sanitation. Food often was inadequate and of poor quality, and many detainees relied on supplemental food, medicines, and warm clothing provided by relatives. Prisoners often reported sleeping on the floor because there were no beds or bedding. In many cases provisions for sanitation, ventilation, heating, lighting, and access to potable water were inadequate.

Adequate, timely medical care for prisoners remained a serious problem, despite official assurances that prisoners have the right to prompt medical treatment. Prison authorities withheld medical treatment from political prisoners. In April prison officials refused requests to send ailing Guangdong activist Yang Maodong (better known by his pen name Guo Feixiong) to a hospital for medical tests. To protest his treatment, he went on a hunger strike, during which prison officials reportedly force-fed him. Guo was also reportedly routinely tortured. In one attempt to humiliate him, prison officials performed a rectal exam on Guo, videotaped the procedure, and threatened to post the video online. In August authorities transferred him to a different prison hospital, and he ended his hunger strike.

Political prisoners were held with the general prison population and reported being beaten by other prisoners at the instigation of guards. Some reported being held in the same cells as death row inmates. Authorities did not allow some dissidents supplemental food, medicine, and warm clothing from relatives.

Conditions in administrative detention facilities were similar to those in prisons. Beating deaths occurred in administrative detention facilities. Detainees reported beatings, sexual assaults, lack of proper food, and limited or no access to medical care.

<u>Administration</u>: Authorities used alternatives to incarceration for both violent and nonviolent offenders. According to the State Council's 2016 *White Paper on Legal Rights*, 2.7 million individuals participated in community correction, with an estimated 689,000 individuals in the program as of September. The same source reported an annual increase of 51,000 individuals in community correction programs.

There were no prison ombudsmen per se, but prisoners and detainees are legally entitled to submit complaints to judicial authorities without censorship and request investigation of credible allegations of inhuman conditions. The law states that letters from a prisoner to higher authorities of the prison or to the judicial organs shall be free from examination; it was unclear to what extent the law was implemented. While authorities occasionally investigated credible allegations of inhuman conditions, the results were not documented in a publicly accessible manner. Many prisoners and detainees did not have reasonable access to visitors and could not engage in religious practices.

Independent Monitoring: Information about prisons and various other types of administrative and extralegal detention facilities was considered a state secret, and the government typically did not permit independent monitoring.

Improvements: In August the Supreme People's Procuratorate published data that favored an "education first" approach towards juvenile crime, specifically focusing on counseling over punishment, according to the Dui Hua Foundation. The same figures showed the number of juvenile arrests later dismissed by the court expanded from 26 percent in 2014 to 29 percent in 2015.

d. Arbitrary Arrest or Detention

Arbitrary arrest and detention remained serious problems. The law grants public security officers broad administrative detention powers and the ability to detain individuals for extended periods without formal arrest or criminal charges. Throughout the year lawyers, human rights activists, journalists, religious leaders, and former political prisoners and their family members continued to be targeted for arbitrary detention or arrest.

Role of the Police and Security Apparatus

The main domestic security agencies include the Ministry of State Security, the Ministry of Public Security, and the People's Armed Police. The People's Liberation Army is primarily responsible for external security but also has some domestic security responsibilities. Local jurisdictions also frequently used civilian municipal security forces, known as "urban management" officials, to enforce administrative measures. Oversight of these forces was localized and ad hoc. By law officials can be criminally prosecuted for abuses of power, but such cases were rarely pursued.

The Ministry of Public Security coordinates the civilian police force, which is organized into specialized agencies and local, county, and provincial jurisdictions. Procuratorate oversight of the public security forces was limited. Corruption at every level was widespread. Public security and urban management officials engaged in extrajudicial detention, extortion, and assault.

Regulations state that officers in prisons face dismissal if found to have beaten, applied corporal punishment, or abused inmates or to have instigated such acts, but there were no reports these regulations were enforced.

In the absence of reliable data, it was difficult to ascertain the full extent of impunity for the domestic security apparatus, but anecdotal accounts of abuse were common on social media and sometimes appeared in state media reports as well. Authorities often announced investigations following cases of reported killings by police. It remained unclear, however, whether these investigations resulted in findings of police malfeasance or disciplinary action.

Arrest Procedures and Treatment of Detainees

Criminal detention beyond 37 days requires approval of a formal arrest by the procuratorate, but in cases pertaining to "national security, terrorism, and major bribery," the law permits up to six months of incommunicado detention without formal arrest. After formally arresting a suspect, public security authorities are authorized to detain a suspect for up to an additional seven months while the case is investigated.

After the completion of an investigation, the procuratorate can detain a suspect an additional 45 days while determining whether to file criminal charges. If charges are filed, authorities can detain a suspect for an additional 45 days before beginning judicial proceedings. Public security sometimes detained persons beyond the period allowed by law, and pretrial detention periods of a year or longer were common.

The law stipulates that detainees be allowed to meet with defense counsel before criminal charges are filed. Some criminal defense attorneys stated that under the 2013 revised criminal procedure law, their ability to meet with clients improved. In some routine cases, defense attorneys could arrange visits at any time and have private meetings with their clients in detention centers. This generally did not apply to cases considered politically sensitive.

The criminal procedure law requires a court to provide a lawyer to a defendant who has not already retained one, who has various disabilities or is a minor, or who faces a life sentence or the death penalty. This law applies whether or not the defendant is indigent. Courts may also provide lawyers to other criminal defendants who cannot afford them, although courts often did not do so.

Criminal defendants are entitled to apply for bail (also translated as "a guarantor pending trial") while awaiting trial, but the system did not appear to operate effectively, and authorities released few suspects on bail.

The law requires notification of family members within 24 hours of detention, but authorities often held individuals without providing such notification for significantly longer periods, especially in politically sensitive cases. In some cases notification did not occur. Under a sweeping exception, officials are not required to provide notification if doing so would "hinder the investigation" of a case. The revised criminal procedure law limits this exception to cases involving state security or terrorism, but public security officials have broad discretion to interpret what is "state security."

The law allows for residential surveillance rather than detention in a formal facility under certain circumstances. With the approval of the next higher-level authorities, officials may place a suspect under "residential surveillance" at a designated place of residence (i.e., a place other than the suspect's home) for up to six months when they suspect crimes of endangering state security, terrorism, or serious bribery and believe that surveillance at the suspect's home would impede the investigation. Human rights organizations and detainees themselves reported that this practice left detainees at a high risk for torture. Authorities may also prevent defense lawyers from meeting with suspects in these categories of cases.

The law provides for the right to petition the government for resolution of grievances, but many citizens who traveled to Beijing to petition the central government were subjected to arbitrary detention, often by security agents dispatched from the petitioner's hometown. Petitioners reported harsh treatment by security officials. In February officers from the Fuyou Street Station of the Xicheng District Public Security Bureau in Beijing reportedly beat Qiao Zhigang, the leader of a group of retired and disabled members of the military, and detained many others who had gathered with Qiao to protest the government's failure to provide promised benefits and compensation.

Authorities used administrative detention to intimidate political and religious activists and to prevent public demonstrations. Forms of administrative detention included compulsory drug rehabilitation treatment (for drug users), "custody and training" (for minor criminal offenders), and "legal education" centers for political and religious activists, particularly Falun Gong practitioners. The maximum stay in compulsory drug rehabilitation centers is two years, including what was generally a six-month stay in a detoxification center.

Arbitrary Arrest: Authorities detained or arrested persons on allegations of revealing state secrets, subversion, and other crimes as a means to suppress political dissent and public advocacy. These charges--including what constitutes a state secret--remained ill defined, and any piece of information could be retroactively designated a state secret. Authorities also used the vaguely worded charges of "picking quarrels and provoking trouble" broadly against many civil rights activists. It remained unclear what this term means. Authorities also detained citizens and foreigners under broad and ambiguous state secret laws for, among other actions, disclosing information on criminal trials, meetings, commercial activity, and government activity. Authorities sometimes retroactively labeled a particular action as a violation of state secret laws. A counterespionage law grants authorities the power to require individuals and organizations to cease any activities deemed a threat to national security. Failure to comply could result in seizure of property and assets.

There were multiple reports of lawyers, petitioners, and other rights activists being arrested or detained for lengthy periods of time, only to have the charges later dismissed for lack of evidence. Many activists were subjected to extralegal house arrest, denied travel rights, or administratively detained in different types of facilities, including "black jails." In some cases public security officials put pressure on schools not to allow the children of prominent political detainees to enroll. Conditions faced by those under house arrest varied but sometimes included isolation in their homes under guard by security agents. Security officials were frequently stationed inside the homes. Authorities placed many citizens under house arrest during sensitive times, such as during the visits of senior foreign government officials or preceding the annual plenary sessions of the National People's Congress, the G20 summit, the anniversary of the Tiananmen massacre, and sensitive anniversaries in Tibetan areas and the XUAR. Some of those not placed under house arrest were taken by security agents to remote areas on so-called forced vacations.

In early September security officials abducted rights lawyer Li Yuhan from the hospital where she was receiving treatment for a heart condition and beat and choked her when she resisted. She was told she would need to take a "vacation" before the G20 Summit to ensure she did not cause trouble. She was held overnight at an undisclosed location, where security officials denied her access to the bathroom. She was released the next day without charges.

Despite being released from prison in 2011, activist Hu Jia remained under extrajudicial house arrest during the year. Human rights lawyer Gao Zhisheng, who was released from prison in 2014, remained confined under strict house arrest.

Pretrial Detention: Pretrial detention could last longer than one year. Defendants in "sensitive cases" reported being subjected to prolonged pretrial detention. Many of the "709" detainees were held in pretrial detention for more than a year without access to their families or their lawyers.

e. Denial of Fair Public Trial

Although the law states that the courts shall exercise judicial power independently, without interference from administrative organs, social organizations, and individuals, the judiciary did not, in fact, exercise judicial power independently. Judges regularly received political guidance on pending cases, including instructions on how to rule, from both the government and the CCP, particularly in politically sensitive cases. The CCP Central Political and Legal Affairs Commission has the authority to review and direct court operations at all levels of the judiciary. All judicial and procuratorate appointments require approval by the CCP Organization Department.

Corruption often influenced court decisions, since safeguards against judicial corruption were vague and poorly enforced. Local governments appointed and paid local court judges and, as a result, often exerted influence over the rulings of those judges.

A CCP-controlled committee decided most major cases, and the duty of trial and appellate court judges was to craft a legal justification for the committee's decision.

Courts are not authorized to rule on the constitutionality of legislation. The law permits organizations or individuals to question the constitutionality of laws and regulations, but a constitutional challenge may be directed only to the promulgating legislative body. Lawyers had little or no opportunity to rely on constitutional claims in litigation.

Media sources indicated public security authorities used televised confessions of lawyers, foreign and domestic bloggers, journalists, and business executives in an attempt to establish guilt before their criminal trial proceedings began or as a method of negotiating release from detention, such as the televised statements of Wang Yu, Zhang Kai, and Swedish national Peter Dahlin. NGOs asserted such statements were likely coerced, perhaps by torture, and some detainees who confessed recanted upon release and confirmed that their confessions had been coerced. No provision in the law allows the pretrial broadcast of confessions by criminal suspects.

"Judicial independence" remained one of the reportedly off-limit subjects that the CCP ordered university professors not to discuss (see section 2.a., Academic Freedom and Cultural Events).

Trial Procedures

Although the amended criminal procedure law reaffirms the presumption of innocence, the criminal justice system remained biased toward a presumption of guilt, especially in high-profile or politically sensitive cases. According to the March work report submitted to the National People's Congress (NPC) by the Supreme People's Court (SPC), more than 1.2 million individuals were convicted while 1,039 were acquitted in 2015. The low acquittal rate of less than 1 percent has persisted for many years, although the overall number of acquittals during the year rose from the 778 recorded in 2014.

In many politically sensitive trials, courts announced guilty verdicts immediately following proceedings with little time for deliberation. Courts often punished defendants who refused to acknowledge guilt with harsher sentences than those who confessed. The appeals process rarely reversed convictions and failed to provide sufficient avenues for review; remedies for violations of defendants' rights were inadequate.

Regulations of the SPC require trials to be open to the public, with the exception of cases involving state secrets, privacy issues, minors, or, on the application of a party to the proceedings, commercial secrets. Authorities used the state secrets provision to keep politically sensitive proceedings closed to the public, sometimes even to family members, and to withhold defendant's access to defense counsel.

Court regulations state that foreigners with valid identification should be allowed to observe trials under the same criteria as citizens, but foreigners were permitted to attend court proceedings only by invitation. As in past years, authorities barred foreign diplomats and journalists from attending a number of trials. In some instances the trials were reclassified as "state secrets" cases or otherwise closed to the public. During the year foreign diplomats attempted to attend at least a dozen public trials throughout the country. In many instances court officials claimed there were no available seats in the courtroom.

Portions of some trials were broadcast, and court proceedings were a regular television feature. In September, Zhou Qiang, the president of the SPC and head of the judiciary, announced the debut of a website, the Chinese Open Trial Network. It offered videos of more than 67,000 criminal, administrative, and civil proceedings, including all open SPC hearings and some select lower court hearings. The CCP leadership of the court involved, however, must approve the streaming of every case.

In keeping with the CCP Central Committee's Fourth Plenum decision to reform certain aspects of the judicial system, the SPC issued updated regulations requiring the release of court judgments online. The regulations, which took effect on October 1, stipulate that court officials should release judgments, with the exception of those involving state secrets and juvenile suspects, within seven days of their adoption. These reforms, aimed at bringing greater transparency to the judicial system, extended to some of the most sensitive political cases. The Dui Hua Foundation reported that it obtained 117 judgments in cases involving state security as of September 30, up from 80 judgments in all of 2015.

Individuals facing administrative detention do not have the right to seek legal counsel. Criminal defendants were eligible for legal assistance, although the vast majority of criminal defendants went to trial without a lawyer. According to the State Council's 2016 *White Paper on Legal Rights*, 4.7 million cases received legal aid from 2012 to 2015.

Lawyers are required to be members of the CCP-controlled All China Lawyers Association, and the Ministry of Justice requires all lawyers to pledge their loyalty to the leadership of the CCP upon issuance or renewal of their license to practice law. The CCP continued to require law firms with three or more party members to form a CCP unit within the firm.

According to Chinese legal experts and statistics reported in domestic media, defense attorneys took part in less than 20 percent of criminal cases; in some provinces it was less than 12 percent. In particular human rights lawyers reported that authorities did not permit them to effectively defend certain clients or threatened them with punishment if they chose to do so. Some lawyers declined to represent defendants in politically sensitive cases, and such defendants frequently found it difficult to find an attorney. When defendants were able to retain counsel in politically sensitive cases, government officials often prevented attorneys from organizing an effective defense. In some instances authorities prevented attorneys selected by defendants from taking the case and appointed a court attorney to the case instead.

Tactics employed by court and government officials included unlawful detentions, disbarment, harassment and physical intimidation, and denial of access to evidence and to clients. In June police beat Guangxi lawyer Wu Liangshu for refusing a body search by court police when he filed a lawsuit with the People's Court in Nanning. Police suspected he was recording their conversations in court. Wu emerged from the courthouse partially stripped with his clothes torn.

The government suspended or revoked the business licenses or law licenses of those who took on sensitive cases, such as defending prodemocracy dissidents, house-church activists, Falun Gong practitioners, or government critics. Authorities used the annual licensing review process administered by the All China Lawyers Association to withhold or delay the renewal of professional lawyers' licenses. In April lawyer Pu Zhiqiang was formally disbarred following the three-year suspended prison term he was given in December 2015 for his online comments critical of CCP rule.

In 2015 the NPC's Standing Committee amended legislation concerning the legal profession. The amendments criminalize attorneys' actions that "insult, defame, or threaten judicial officers," "do not heed the court's admonition," or "severely disrupt courtroom order." The changes also criminalize disclosing client or case information to media outlets or using protests, the media, or other means to influence court decisions. Violators face fines and up to three years in prison.

Regulations adopted in 2015 also state that detention center officials should either allow defense attorneys to meet suspects or defendants or explain why the meeting cannot be arranged at that time. The regulations specify that a meeting should be arranged within 48 hours. Procuratorates and courts should allow defense attorneys to access and read case files within three working days. The time and frequency of opportunities available for defense attorneys to read case files shall not be limited, according to the guidelines. In some sensitive cases, lawyers had no pretrial access to their clients, and defendants and lawyers were not allowed to communicate with one another during trials. In contravention of the revised criminal procedure law (see section 1.d.), criminal defendants frequently were not assigned an attorney until a case was brought to court. The law stipulates the spoken and written language of criminal proceedings shall be conducted in the language common to the specific locality, with government interpreters providing language services for defendants not proficient in the local language. Sources noted that trials were predominantly conducted in Mandarin Chinese even in minority areas with interpreters provided for defendants who did not speak the language.

Mechanisms allowing defendants to confront their accusers were inadequate. Only a small percentage of trials reportedly involved witnesses. Judges retained significant discretion over whether live witness testimony was required or even allowed. In most criminal trials, prosecutors read witness statements, which neither the defendants nor their lawyers had an opportunity to rebut through cross-examination. Although the law states that pretrial witness statements cannot serve as the sole basis for conviction, prosecutors relied heavily on such statements. Defense attorneys had no authority to compel witnesses to testify or to mandate discovery, although they could apply for access to government-held evidence relevant to their case.

In 2015 the Ministry of Justice announced a rule that requires assigning lawyers to convicted prisoners on death row who cannot afford one during the review of their sentences. The number of capital offenses in the criminal code was reduced to 46 in 2015. Official figures on executions were classified as a state secret. According to the Dui Hua Foundation, the number of executions fell to 2,400 in 2013, down from a high of 24,000 in 1983. The drop reflected the reform of the capital punishment system initiated in 2007, but the number of executions since 2013 stabilized or even increased. Dui Hua also reported that an increase in the number of Uighur executions likely offset the drop in the number of Han Chinese executed.

Political Prisoners and Detainees

Government officials continued to deny holding any political prisoners, asserting that persons were detained not for their political or religious views but because they violated the law. Authorities, however, continued to imprison citizens for reasons related to politics and religion. Tens of thousands of political prisoners remained incarcerated, most in prisons and some in administrative detention. The government did not grant international humanitarian organizations access to political prisoners.

Political prisoners were granted early release at lower rates than other prisoners. The Dui Hua Foundation estimated that more than 100 prisoners were still serving sentences for counterrevolution and hooliganism, two crimes removed from the criminal code in 1997. Thousands of others were serving sentences for political and religious offenses, including "endangering state security" and "cult" offenses covered under Article 300 of the criminal code, crimes introduced in 1997. The government neither reviewed the cases of those charged before 1997 with counterrevolution and hooliganism nor released persons jailed for nonviolent offenses under repealed provisions.

In August, four men were convicted of the political crime of "subversion of state power" as a result of the 2015 "709" crackdown on public interest legal activism. Zhou Shifeng, the founder of the Beijing Feng Rui Law Firm, was sentenced to seven years for subversion. The media reported that prosecutors stated Zhou had "conspired with foreign governments," and Zhou reportedly confessed to his crimes in a statement that some observers interpreted as a protest of the ruling. As recently as 2012, Beijing municipal authorities honored Zhou with recognition as a "Beijing Excellent Lawyer" for three straight years. His law firm was known for its legal activism and had represented clients in high-profile cases, including the 2008 melamine milk scandal.

In August authorities sentenced democracy activist and unregistered church leader Hu Shigen to seven years in prison for "subversion of state power." The media reported he pled guilty, and his was one of the longer sentences among those detained during the "709" crackdown. In the same week, Feng Rui associate Zhai Yanmin and Christian activist Guo Hongguo were also convicted of the same charges, although both received suspended sentences.

In September the Beijing Municipal No. 2 Intermediate Court sentenced human rights lawyer Xia Lin, who previously represented artist Ai Weiwei, to 12 years' imprisonment on charges of fraud. Supporters said that the charges were baseless and that authorities targeted Xia for his efforts to support human rights activists.

Many political prisoners remained in prison or under other forms of detention at year's end, including writer Yang Maodong (Guo Feixiong); Uighur scholar Ilham Tohti; anticorruption activist Xu Zhiyong; Wang Bingzhang; activist Liu Xianbin;

Zhou Yongjun; online dissident Kong Youping; Roman Catholic bishops Ma Daqin and Su Zhimin; pastor Zhang Shaojie; Falun Gong practitioner Bian Lichao; lawyers or legal associates Li Heping, Wang Quanzhang, Xie Yanyi, Xie Yang, and Li Chunfu; blogger Wu Gan; and many others. Nobel Peace Prize laureate Liu Xiaobo remained in Jinzhou Prison in Liaoning Province. His wife, Liu Xia, remained under surveillance and faced continued restrictions on her freedom of movement.

Criminal punishments included "deprivation of political rights" for a fixed period after release from prison, during which an individual could be denied rights of free speech, association, and publication. Former prisoners reported that their ability to find employment, travel, obtain residence permits and passports, rent residences, and access social services was severely restricted.

Authorities frequently subjected former political prisoners and their families to surveillance, telephone wiretaps, searches, and other forms of harassment or threats. For example, security personnel followed the family members of detained or imprisoned rights activists to meetings with foreign reporters and diplomats and urged the family members to remain silent about the cases of their relatives. Certain members of the rights community were barred from meeting with visiting dignitaries.

According to the 2015 *China Law Yearbook*, in 2014 authorities indicted 1,411 individuals for "endangering state security," an increase of 2 percent from 2013. Based on figures in the report of the Supreme People's Court to the 2016 plenary session of the National People's Congress, the Dui Hua Foundation estimated that approximately 500 "endangering state security" trials took place in 2015, down from approximately 1,000 in 2014, a decline believed to be due to the reclassification of crimes. Offenses previously considered as "endangering state security" were, starting in 2015, increasingly dealt with as "terrorism" and "disturbing social order," including a charge frequently used against activists called "picking quarrels and provoking trouble."

Civil Judicial Procedures and Remedies

Courts deciding civil matters faced the same limitations on judicial independence as criminal courts. The State Compensation Law provides administrative and judicial remedies for plaintiffs whose rights or interests government agencies or officials have infringed. The law also allows compensation for wrongful detention, mental trauma, or physical injuries inflicted by detention center or prison officials.

Citizens seldom applied for state compensation because of the high cost of bringing lawsuits, low credibility of courts, and citizens' lack of awareness of the law. Victims' claims were difficult to assess because of vague definitions in the law and difficulties in obtaining evidence of damage. Judges were reluctant to accept such cases, and government agencies seldom ruled in favor of plaintiffs.

In some cases authorities pressured plaintiffs to drop their lawsuits. On May 1, Chen Wenying dropped her suit against the Xinhua News Agency and China Central Television (CCTV) for allegedly falsely accusing her son, labor rights activist Zeng Feiyang, of committing fraud. Chen decided to withdraw the lawsuit after she and her family began to receive threats from the government.

f. Arbitrary or Unlawful Interference with Privacy, Family, Home, or Correspondence

The law states that the "freedom and privacy of correspondence of citizens are protected by law," but authorities often did not respect the privacy of citizens. Although the law requires warrants before officers can search premises, officials frequently ignored this requirement. The Public Security Bureau and prosecutors are authorized to issue search warrants on their own authority without judicial review. Cases of forced entry by police officers continued to be reported.

Authorities monitored telephone calls, text messages, faxes, e-mail, instant messaging, and other digital communications intended to remain private. They also opened and censored domestic and international mail. Security services routinely monitored and entered residences and offices to gain access to computers, telephones, and fax machines. Foreign journalists leaving the country found some of their personal belongings searched. In some cases, when material deemed politically sensitive was uncovered, the journalists had to sign a statement stating they would "voluntarily" leave these documents behind in China.

In September the General Office of the CCP Central Committee and the PRC State Council issued a directive mandating the establishment of a centralized "social credit system" to evaluate the trustworthiness of all individuals and companies in the country. Each person and company is to be assigned a score on the basis of information collected from the internet as well as public records. The directive's goal is "to construct a credit-monitoring, warning, and punishment system" that operates on the principle that "if trust is broken in one place, restrictions are imposed everywhere." It details a wide range of privileges that could be denied and punishments that could be imposed for "trust-breaking" conduct, including subjecting individuals and companies to targeted daily monitoring, random inspections, and possible arrest and criminal prosecution. The directive requires that an individual's score be considered when he or she attempts to establish a social organization, and it singles out lawyers and law firms for restrictions if they engage in "trust-breaking" conduct.

According to media reports, the Ministry of Public Security used tens of millions of surveillance cameras throughout the country to monitor the general public. In 2015 the Beijing Municipal Public Security Bureau announced it had "covered every corner of the capital with a video surveillance system." Human rights groups stated that authorities increasingly relied on video and other forms of surveillance to monitor and intimidate political dissidents, Tibetans, and Uighurs. The monitoring and disruption of telephone and internet communications were particularly widespread in the XUAR and Tibetan areas. The Cybersecurity Law passed in November codified the authority of security agencies to cut communication networks across an entire geographic region during "major security incidents," although they have previously exercised this authority prior to passage of the Cybersecurity Law.

Forced relocation because of urban development continued in some locations. Protests over relocation terms or compensation were common, and some protest leaders were prosecuted. In rural areas infrastructure and commercial development projects resulted in the forced relocation of thousands of persons.

Property-related disputes between citizens and government authorities sometimes turned violent. These disputes frequently stemmed from local officials' collusion with property developers to pay little or no compensation to displaced residents, combined with a lack of effective government oversight or media scrutiny of local officials' involvement in property transactions as well as a lack of legal remedies or other dispute resolution mechanisms for displaced residents. The problem persisted despite central government claims it had imposed stronger controls over illegal land seizures and taken steps to standardize compensation. Redevelopment in traditional Uighur neighborhoods in cities throughout the XUAR resulted in the destruction of historically or culturally important areas. Some residents expressed opposition to the lack of proper compensation by the government and the coercive measures used to obtain their agreement to redevelopment.

There were several reports of authorities confiscating traditional pastoral lands from ethnic Mongolian herders for development in the Inner Mongolia Autonomous Region. In August authorities in Shin-Barag Left Banner forcibly evicted ethnic Mongolian herders from their pastoral lands they had grazed for generations under a legal contract with the government. Media and private sources reported that paramilitary officers placed the region under a security lockdown and detained 10 herders, charging one named Huubshalat with "separatism."

Section 2. Respect for Civil Liberties, Including:

a. Freedom of Speech and Press

The constitution states that citizens "enjoy freedom of speech, of the press, of assembly, of association, of procession and of demonstration," although authorities generally did not respect these rights, especially when they conflicted with CCP interests. Authorities continued tight control of print, broadcast, and electronic media and regularly used them to propagate government views and CCP ideology. Authorities censored and manipulated the press and the internet, particularly around sensitive anniversaries.

Freedom of Speech and Expression: Citizens could discuss many political topics privately and in small groups without official punishment. The government, however, routinely took harsh action against citizens who questioned the legitimacy of the CCP. Some independent think tanks, study groups, and seminars reported pressure to cancel sessions on sensitive topics. Those who made politically sensitive comments in public speeches, academic discussions, or in remarks to the media remained subject to punitive measures.

In late February prominent real estate developer Ren Zhiqiang criticized President Xi's call for media outlets to display absolute loyalty to the CCP. In two social media posts, Ren urged the CCP not to waste taxpayer money and opined, "Since when did the people's government become the party's government?" The government consequently stripped Ren Zhiqiang of his social media accounts, which had an estimated 37 million followers. The *New York Times* reported on March 11 that Xinhua News Agency employee Zhou Gang issued an online letter accusing government censors of silencing critics, apparently in response to the Ren case.

Two weeks after President Xi's visit to state media, anonymous authors posted a letter online calling for him to resign "for the future of the country and the people." The authors claimed to be "loyal Communist Party members." Authorities promptly shut down *Wujie News*, the news website that carried the letter, and detained journalists, such as Jia Jia, whom security agents apprehended at the

Beijing airport en route to Hong Kong. According to contacts and news reports, all *Wujie News* staff were later released.

In April online commentator Tian Li (also known as Chen Qitang) was tried for "inciting subversion of state power." His verdict was suspended for a third time, with no announcement made before the end of the year. The charges stemmed from six political commentaries Chen had posted, three of which he had personally written. The prosecution said the articles represented a "harsh attack" on the CCP.

In November, Liu Feiyue, the founder of the Civil Rights and Livelihood Watch website, was detained on charges of "inciting state subversion" in Hubei Province. He had been detained and released earlier in the year when he tried to cover the CCP Central Committee's sixth plenary session in Beijing.

Huang Qi, founder of the Tianwang Human Rights Center, was detained on November 28 and formally charged with "illegally providing state secrets abroad" on December 16. Authorities had long taken action against Huang for his efforts to document human rights abuses in the country on his 64Tianwang.com website. Previously convicted of "inciting subversion of state power" and "illegally possessing state secrets" in 2003 and 2008, he served five and three years in prison, respectively.

Press and Media Freedoms: The CCP and government continued to maintain ultimate authority over all published, online, or broadcast material. Officially, only state-run media outlets have government approval to cover CCP leaders or other topics deemed "sensitive." While it did not dictate all content to be published or broadcast, the CCP and the government had unchecked authority to mandate if, when, and how particular issues were reported or to order that they not be reported at all.

The government continued to strictly monitor the press and media, including film and television, via its broadcast and press regulatory body, the State Administration of Press, Publication, Radio, Film, and Television (SAPPRFT). The Cyberspace Administration of China (CAC) regulates online news media. All books and magazines continued to require state-issued publication numbers, which were expensive and often difficult to obtain. As in the past, nearly all print and broadcast media as well as book publishers were affiliated with the CCP or government. There were a small number of print publications with some private ownership interest but no privately owned television or radio stations. There were growing numbers of privately owned online media. The CCP directed the domestic media to refrain from reporting on certain subjects, and traditional broadcast programming required government approval. The SAPPRFT announced that satellite television channels may broadcast no more than two imported television programs each year during prime-time hours and that imported programs must receive the approval of local regulators at least two months in advance.

In a well-publicized February 19 visit to the three main state and CCP news organizations--the Xinhua News Agency, CCTV, and the *People's Daily*--President Xi said, "Party and state-run media are the propaganda battlefield of the party and the government, [and] must bear the surname of the party. All of the party's news and public opinion work must embody the party's will, reflect the party's ideas, defend the authority of the Party Central Committee, [and] defend the unity of the party."

In March the prominent Chinese financial magazine *Caixin* defied the government by highlighting censorship of its online content. On March 5, *Caixin* published an article pointing out how the CAC had deleted an interview with Jiang Hong, a delegate to the advisory Chinese People's Political Consultative Conference, because it touched on the issue of free speech. The CAC told *Caixin* editors the interview contained "illegal content" and "violated laws and regulations."

Both the SAPPRFT and CAC continued efforts to reassert control over the country's growing world of new media. In December the SAPPRFT announced that commercial social media platforms like WeChat and Weibo are not allowed to disseminate user-generated audio or video programs about current events and are only supposed to distribute content from those that hold state-issued audiovisual online transmission licenses.

<u>Violence and Harassment</u>: The government frequently impeded the work of the press, including citizen journalists. Journalists reported being subjected to physical attack, harassment, and intimidation when reporting on sensitive topics. Government officials used criminal prosecution, civil lawsuits, and other punishment, including violence, detention, and other forms of harassment, to intimidate authors and journalists and to prevent the dissemination of unsanctioned information on a wide range of topics. A journalist could face demotion or job loss for publishing views that challenged the government.

Family members of journalists based overseas also faced harassment, and in some cases detention, as retaliation for the reporting of their relatives abroad. In March authorities detained the siblings of the Germany-based writer Zhang Ping after he wrote an article criticizing the government for its role in the disappearance of journalist Jia Jia. The family members, detained in Xichong County, Sichuan Province, were released several days later, and Zhang later publicly said he had "cut off ties" in order to protect them.

Uighur webmasters Dilshat Perhat and Nijat Azat continued to serve sentences for "endangering state security." During the year additional journalists working in traditional and new media were also imprisoned.

Liu Yuxia, front-page editor of the *Southern Metropolis Daily*, once considered a bastion for relatively independent views, was dismissed in March after the headline of one of the newspaper's front-page stories about the burial of a prominent reformer was seen as a veiled criticism of President Xi's admonition that the media "bear the surname of the party." If the Chinese characters of the headline about the sea burial were read vertically in conjunction with the headline about President Xi's call for loyalty by the media, as both headlines appeared in proximity on the same page, the combined headline could be interpreted as "the souls of Chinese media have died because they bear the party's name."

Li Xin, another former editor for the *Southern Metropolis Daily*'s website, disappeared in Thailand and reappeared in China under detention after reportedly seeking political asylum in Thailand. Yu Shaolei, who edited the newspaper's cultural section, also resigned in late March. Yu reportedly posted a photograph of his resignation form on Weibo, citing his "inability to bear your surname." One *Southern Metropolis Daily* journalist was quoted as stating, "We think it won't get any worse and then it does. We are being strangled."

Four of the five Hong Kong booksellers who disappeared between October and December 2015 were released but remained under surveillance (see section 1.b.). In June, Zhu Tiezhi, the deputy editor in chief of *Qiushi*, the CCP's foremost theoretical journal, reportedly hanged himself in the garage of the building where the journal was housed. Media outlets reported that Zhu had been depressed by ideological infighting within the CCP and was linked to Ling Jihua, one of former president Hu Jintao's closest aides, who became a prime target in President Xi's anticorruption campaign.

In December security officials in Gannan County, Heilongjiang Province, detained and beat journalists Liu Bozhi and Liu Dun from *China Educational News* after they investigated reports of financial irregularities in public school cafeterias.

In July the state-controlled Chinese Academy of National Arts announced on its website that it had removed the existing management of the monthly magazine *Yanhuang Chunqiu*, including its 93-year-old publisher and cofounder Du Daozheng. The magazine was known as an "intellectual oasis" in which topics like democracy and other "sensitive" issues could be discussed, and it had a reputation for publishing views on politics and history that challenged CCP orthodoxy. Observers saw the removal of Du along with several other senior staff including Hu Dehua, the son of late reformist CCP leader Hu Yaobang, as a threat to one of the country's last strongholds of liberal thought. The magazine's chief editor Yang Jisheng quit in 2015 in protest of increasing censorship. Following the forced reshuffle, Du suspended the publication on July 19, and it had not resumed operations by year's end.

In September journalists were attacked, detained, and expelled from Wukan, a fishing village in Guangdong Province, as they tried to conduct interviews following protests over alleged land seizures and the detention of the elected village chief. Wukan was the site of protests in 2011 over land seizures and corruption, to which the provincial government responded by allowing villagers to elect their local leader.

Foreign journalists based in the country continued to face a challenging environment for reporting. According to the annual *Reporting Conditions* survey of the Foreign Correspondents' Club of China (FCCC) conducted during the year, 98 percent of respondents did not believe reporting conditions in the country met international standards. In addition, 48 percent of respondents believed working conditions had stayed the same since the previous year, while 29 percent believed conditions had deteriorated. Fifty-seven percent said they had been subjected to some form of interference, harassment, or violence while attempting to report from the country.

Restrictions on foreign journalists by central and local CCP propaganda departments remained strict, especially during sensitive times and anniversaries. Foreign press outlets reported that local employees of foreign news agencies were also subjected to official harassment and intimidation and that this remained a major concern for foreign outlets. The FCCC's survey reported that 26 percent of respondents described interference or obstruction by police or "unidentified individuals" while reporting. Eight percent of respondents reported being subjected to "manhandling or physical violence," a 3 percent increase from 2015. In addition, FCCC members reported physical and electronic surveillance of their staff and premises.

Although authorities continued to use the registration and renewal of residency visas and foreign ministry press cards to pressure and punish journalists whose reporting perturbed authorities, wait times were reportedly shorter for many applicants than in previous years. Many foreign media organizations continued to have trouble expanding their operations in the country due to the difficulty of receiving visas for new positions. Government officials continued to require regular meetings with journalists at the time of their renewals or after seeing reports they deemed "sensitive," at which officials commonly made clear to reporters they were under scrutiny for their reporting. Security personnel often visited reporters unannounced and questioned them about their reporting activities.

Authorities continued to enforce tight restrictions on citizens employed by foreign news organizations. The code of conduct for citizen employees of foreign media organizations threatens dismissal and loss of accreditation for those citizen employees who engage in independent reporting. It instructs them to provide their employers information that projects "a good image of the country." Several FCCC members reported local assistants had been summoned for meetings with security officials that the assistants found extremely intimidating. One foreign correspondent said security officials had called her local assistant a "traitor" and asked her why she was willing to help the foreign press with its "anti-China bias."

Media outlets that reported on commercial issues enjoyed comparatively fewer restrictions, but the system of postpublication review by propaganda officials encouraged self-censorship by editors seeking to avoid the losses associated with penalties for inadvertently printing unauthorized content.

Censorship or Content Restrictions: The State Council's Regulations on the Administration of Publishing grant broad authority to the government at all levels to restrict publications based on content, including mandating if, when, and how particular issues are reported. While the Ministry of Foreign Affairs daily press briefing was generally open, and the State Council Information Office organized some briefings by other government agencies, journalists did not have free access to other media events. The Ministry of Defense continued allowing select foreign media outlets to attend monthly press briefings.

Official guidelines for domestic journalists were often vague, subject to change at the discretion of propaganda officials, and enforced retroactively. Propaganda authorities forced newspapers to fire editors and journalists responsible for articles deemed inconsistent with official policy and suspended or closed publications.

Self-censorship remained prevalent among journalists, authors, and editors, particularly with post facto government reviews carrying penalties of ranging severity.

The CCP Central Propaganda Department ordered media outlets to adhere strictly to the information provided by authoritative official departments when reporting on officials suspected of involvement in graft or bribery. Throughout the year the Central Propaganda Department issued similar instructions regarding various prominent events. Directives often warned against reporting on issues related to party and official reputation, health and safety, and foreign affairs. The orders included instructions for media outlets not to investigate or report on their own. The CAC and SAPPRFT strengthened regulations over the content online publications are allowed to distribute, reiterating long-standing rules that only state-licensed news media may conduct original reporting.

The FCCC reported that it was still largely impossible for foreign journalists to report from the TAR, other Tibetan areas, or Xinjiang without experiencing serious interference. Those who took part in government-sponsored trips to the TAR and other Tibetan areas expressed dissatisfaction with the access provided. Of those who tried to report from Tibetan areas, 60 percent reported problems, while 44 percent had trouble in Xinjiang. Foreign reporters also experienced restricted access and interference when trying to report in other sensitive areas, including the North Korean border, coal mining sites where protests had taken place, and other sites of social unrest, such as Wukan village in Guangdong Province.

Authorities continued to jam, with varying degrees of success, Chinese-, Uighur-, and Tibetan-language broadcasts of the Voice of America (VOA), the BBC, and Radio Free Asia. English-language VOA broadcasts generally were not jammed. Internet distribution of streaming radio news and podcasts from these sources was often blocked. Despite the jamming of overseas broadcasts, the VOA, the BBC, Radio Free Asia, Deutsche Welle, and Radio France International had large audiences, including human rights advocates, ordinary citizens, and government officials.

Overseas television newscasts, largely restricted to hotels and foreign residence compounds, were occasionally subject to censorship. Individual issues of foreign newspapers and magazines occasionally were banned when they contained articles deemed too sensitive.

Politically sensitive coverage in Chinese, and to a lesser extent in English, was censored more than coverage in other languages. The government prohibited some foreign and domestic films deemed too sensitive or selectively censored parts of films before they were released.

In November the NPC Standing Committee passed a Cybersecurity Law containing a provision that appeared to be aimed at deterring economists and journalists from publishing analysis that deviated from official views on the economy. Article 12 of the law criminalizes using the internet to "fabricate or spread false information to disturb economic order." In January authorities blocked Reuters' social media account on the Chinese platform Sina Weibo following a report that the country's securities regulator Xiao Gang had offered to resign. The government stated that the Reuters report was not accurate, but a month later state media announced Xiao had been forced out.

Authorities continued to ban books with content they deemed inconsistent with officially sanctioned views. The law permits only government-approved publishing houses to print books. The SAPPRFT controlled all licenses to publish. Newspapers, periodicals, books, audio and video recordings, or electronic publications could not be printed or distributed without SAPPRFT approval and relevant provincial publishing authorities. Individuals who attempted to publish without government approval faced imprisonment, fines, confiscation of their books, and other sanctions. The CCP also exerted control over the publishing industry by preemptively classifying certain topics as state secrets.

Many intellectuals and scholars exercised self-censorship, anticipating that books or papers on political topics would be deemed too sensitive to be published.

Actions to Expand Press Freedom: The Ministry of Foreign Affairs began implementing a new system for journalist visa renewals and press card issuance. There were few complaints, but there was insufficient evidence to comment on the situation at the year's end. Delays persisted in the approval process to expand foreign bureaus as well as visa applications for short-term reporting tours.

Internet Freedom

The internet continued to be widely available and used. According to an official report released in August by the China Internet Network Information Center, the country had 710 million internet users, accounting for 51.7 percent of its total population. The report noted 21.3 million new internet users in the first half of the year, with approximately 191 million going online from rural areas. Major media companies estimated that more than 500 million persons, mainly urban residents, obtained their news from social and online media sources. According to the 2016 *Chinese Media Blue Book*, online media organizations accounted for 47 percent of the country's entire media industry.

Although the internet was widely available, it was heavily censored. The government continued to employ tens of thousands of individuals at the national, provincial, and local levels to monitor electronic communications and online content. The government also reportedly paid personnel to promote official views on various websites and social media and to combat those who posted alternative views. Internet companies also employed thousands of censors to carry out CCP and government injunctions.

During the year there was a steady stream of new regulatory efforts to tighten government control of the online media space that had grown rapidly in the last four years, including draft regulations on strengthening government control of internet news services and online publishing.

The government's updated definition of "internet news information" includes all matters pertaining to politics, economics, defense, diplomacy and "other social public issues and reports and comments of breaking social events." Draft regulations require that all news reports conform to official views, establish a "dishonesty blacklist" system, and expand criminal penalties for violators.

In June the State Internet Information Office published a *Circular on Further Strengthening the Management and Control of False News*, which prohibits online platforms from publishing unverified content as news reports and strengthens regulation on the editing and distribution of news on online platforms, including microblogs and WeChat. The circular prohibits websites from publishing "hearsay and rumors to fabricate news or distort facts based on speculation."

During the year the State Internet Information Office reportedly strengthened efforts to "punish and correct" false online news, reprimanding numerous popular portals, such as Sina, iFeng, and Caijing, and calling on the public to help monitor and report on "illegal and harmful information" found online.

On June 25, the CAC released *New Regulations on Internet Searches* that took effect August 1. The regulations specifically ban search engines from showing "subversive" content and obscene information, longstanding prohibitions for local website operators.

On June 28, the CAC released new *Regulations on the Administration of Mobile Internet App Services* that also took effect on August 1. The new rules expand the application of some requirements to app stores, such as Apple's iTunes App Store, and developers and require mobile app providers to verify users' identities with real-name registration, improve censorship, and punish users who spread "illicit information" on their platforms. The rules prescribe broad and vaguely worded prohibitions on content that "endangers national security," "damages the honor or interests of the state," "propagates cults or superstition," or "harms social ethics or any fine national culture or traditions." At year's end authorities required Apple to remove the *New York Times* English- and Chinese-language news apps from its iTunes App Store in the country. At least three apps were known to have been blocked since April.

In August the CAC called for an "editor in chief" system, ensuring that senior staff are responsible for online editorial decisions contrary to the government's wishes or censorship guidelines. In September media outlets also reported the CAC had launched a campaign to clean up the comments sections on websites, which a CAC official described as an effort to make it easier for individuals to report illegal or harmful content.

In April, GreatFire.org, a website run by activists tracking online censorship in the country, reported that 21 percent of more than 40,000 domains, web links, social media searches, and internet protocol addresses that it monitors in the country were blocked. In addition to social media websites such as Facebook, the government continued to block almost all access to Google websites, including its e-mail service, photograph program, map service, calendar application, and YouTube.

Government censors continued to block websites or online content related to topics deemed sensitive, such as Taiwan, the Dalai Lama, Tibet, the 1989 Tiananmen massacre, and all content related to the Panama Papers. The *Economist*, for example, was blocked in April after it printed an article critical of President Xi's consolidation of power. Many other websites for international media outlets, such as the *New York Times*, the *Wall Street Journal*, and *Bloomberg*, remained perennially blocked, in addition to human rights websites, such as those of Amnesty International and Human Rights Watch.

Authorities continued to jail numerous internet writers for their peaceful expression of political views. In June authorities in Yunnan Province detained citizen journalists Lu Yuyu and Li Tingyu on suspicion of "picking quarrels and provoking trouble" as a result of their reporting. Li and Lu compiled and catalogued daily lists of "mass incidents"--the official term for protests, demonstrations, and riots--and disseminated their findings to the public via social media platforms, such as Weibo. Public security officials reportedly beat Lu, choked him, and twisted his arms until he was badly bruised. Reporters without Borders stated that Lu and Li were among 80 detained citizen journalists and bloggers.

In addition, there continued to be reports of cyberattacks against foreign websites, journalists, and media organizations carrying information that the government restricted internet users from accessing. As in the past, the government selectively blocked access to sites operated by foreign governments, including instances involving the website or social media platforms of health organizations, educational institutions, NGOs, and social networking sites as well as search engines.

While such censorship was effective in keeping casual users away from websites hosting sensitive content, some users circumvented online censorship through the use of various technologies. Information on proxy servers outside the country and software for defeating official censorship were available inside the country, but the government increasingly blocked access to the websites and proxy servers of commercial, academic, and other virtual private network providers.

The State Secrets Law obliges internet companies to cooperate with investigations of suspected leaks of state secrets, stop the transmission of such information once discovered, and report the crime to authorities. Furthermore, the companies must comply with authorities' orders to delete such information from their websites; failure to do so is punishable by relevant departments, such as police and the Ministry of Public Security.

At the World Internet Conference in China in November, Ren Xianling, the vice minister for the CAC, called on participants to embrace state control of the internet and likened such controls to "installing brakes on a car before driving on the road." Xi Jinping opened the conference with a videotaped address in which he reasserted earlier claims that the government exercised absolute control over the internet in the country through "cyber sovereignty."

Academic Freedom and Cultural Events

The government continued restrictions on academic and artistic freedom and on political and social discourse at colleges, universities, and research institutes. Restrictive SAPPRFT and Central Propaganda Department regulations and decisions constrained the flow of ideas and persons. In 2013 the *South China Morning Post* reported that the CCP issued secret instructions to university faculty identifying seven "off-limits" subjects, including universal values, freedom of the press, civil society, civil rights, an independent judiciary, elite cronyism, and the historical errors of the CCP. Some academics self-censored their publications, faced pressure to reach predetermined research results, or were unable to hold conferences with international participants during politically sensitive periods. Foreign academics claimed the government used visa denials, along with blocking access to archives, fieldwork, or interviews, to pressure them to self-censor their work.

In 2015 then minister of education Yuan Guiren restricted the use of foreign textbooks in classrooms. Domestically produced textbooks remained under the editorial control of the CCP. In January, Reuters reported that the CCP Central Commission for Discipline Inspection had set up a team at the Ministry of Education that was "increasing supervision and inspection of political discipline" with the stated purpose, among other things, of preventing CCP members on university campuses from making "irresponsible remarks about major policies." In addition, schools at all levels were required to merge "patriotic education" into their curriculum and extracurricular activities. The government and the CCP Organization Department controlled appointments to most leadership positions at universities, including department heads. While CCP membership was not always a requirement to obtain a tenured faculty position, scholars without CCP affiliation often had fewer chances for promotion.

In July, Chen Baosheng became minister of education, and one of his first acts was to establish a Commission on University Political Education to strengthen ideological discipline within the higher education system. At a press conference in March, Yuan highlighted the centrality of political indoctrination in the education system, declaring "the goal and orientation of running schools is to make our students become people qualified to inherit and build up socialism with Chinese characteristics." The CCP continued to require undergraduate students, regardless of academic major, to complete political ideology coursework on subjects such as Marxism, Maoism, and Deng Xiaoping thought.

In December, Xi Jinping chaired the National Ideology and Political Work Conference for Higher Education and called for turning the academy into a "stronghold that adheres to party leadership." Xi stressed that "China's colleges and universities are institutions of higher learning under the Party's leadership; they are colleges and universities with Chinese socialist characteristics." Xi further asserted that strengthening the role of Marxism in the curriculum was needed to "guide the teachers and students to become staunch believers in the socialist value system." Xi specifically called on professors to become "staunch supporters of the Party's rule."

Authorities on some occasions blocked entry into the country of individuals deemed politically sensitive and frequently refused to issue passports to citizens selected for international exchange programs who were considered "politically unreliable," singling out Tibetans, Uighurs, and individuals from other minority nationality areas. A number of other foreign government-sponsored exchange selectees who already had passports, including some academics, encountered difficulties gaining approval to travel to participate in their programs. Academics reported having to request permission to travel overseas and, in some cases, said they were limited in the number of foreign trips they could take per year.

Censorship and self-censorship of artistic works was common, particularly those artworks deemed to involve politically sensitive subjects. In addition, authorities scrutinized the content of cultural events and applied pressure to encourage self-censorship of discussions. In March a cafe was effectively prevented from a holding an event discussing online censorship in the country after security agents threatened one of the visiting Chinese participants.

b. Freedom of Peaceful Assembly and Association

Freedom of Assembly

While the constitution provides for freedom of peaceful assembly, the government severely restricted this right. The law stipulates that such activities may not challenge "party leadership" or infringe upon the "interests of the state." Protests against the political system or national leaders were prohibited. Authorities denied permits and quickly suppressed demonstrations involving expression of dissenting political views.

The law protects an individual's ability to petition the government, but persons petitioning the government faced restrictions on their rights to assemble and raise grievances (see section 1.d.).

While the central government reiterated prohibitions against blocking or restricting "normal petitioning" and against unlawfully detaining petitioners, official retaliation against petitioners continued. This was partly due to central government regulations that took effect in 2015 requiring local governments to resolve complaints within 60 days and stipulating that central authorities will no longer accept petitions already handled by local or provincial governments. The regulations encourage all litigation-related petitions to be handled at the local level through local or provincial courts, reinforcing a system of incentives for local officials to prevent petitioners from raising complaints to higher levels. It also resulted in local officials sending security personnel to Beijing and forcibly returning petitioners to their home provinces to prevent them from filing complaints against local officials with the central government. Such detentions often went unrecorded and often resulted in brief periods of incarceration in extralegal "black jails."

Petitioners faced harassment, illegal detention, and even more severe forms of punishment when attempting to travel to Beijing to present their grievances.

Citizens throughout the country continued to gather publicly to protest evictions, forced relocations, and inadequate compensation, often resulting in conflict with authorities or other charges.

Although peaceful protests are legal, public security officials rarely granted permits to demonstrate. Despite restrictions, many demonstrations occurred, but those motivated by broad political or social grievances were broken up quickly, sometimes with excessive force.

In June authorities arrested Wukan's popularly elected village mayor, Lin Zuluan, on corruption charges. On September 8, Lin was convicted and sentenced to three years in prison and fined 200,000 yuan ($29,000). Large numbers of villagers took to the streets to protest what they considered bogus charges brought against Lin because of his resistance to land confiscation by higher-level authorities. Authorities deployed large numbers of riot police and used tear gas and rubber bullets to disperse the protest. Public security forces reportedly beat villagers at random, forcibly entered private homes to detain individuals suspected of participating in the protests, and prevented anyone from entering or leaving the village. The authorities also reportedly detained, interrogated, and assaulted foreign journalists, offering rewards for information leading to their detention. At year's end dozens of villagers remained in detention, and at least 13 individuals suspected of leading the protest had been charged with crimes.

In July, thousands of citizens took to the streets in Lubu to protest plans for a new incinerator plant. Local citizens were concerned the plant would contaminate drinking water. The BBC reported that 21 protest leaders were detained, and other media reports indicated that the protests turned violent.

Rights lawyers and activists who advocated for nonviolent civil disobedience were detained, arrested, and in some cases sentenced to prison terms. In January a Guangzhou court convicted Tang Jingling, Yuan Xinting, and Wang Qingying of "inciting subversion of state power," citing their promotion of civil disobedience and the peaceful transition to democratic rule as evidence. Media outlets reported the men were also signatories of the Charter 08 manifesto advocating political reform.

In April human rights activist Su Changlan stood trial at Foshan Intermediate Court on charges of "incitement to subvert state power" for activities in support of the 2014 Hong Kong prodemocracy movement. Five activists who gathered outside the court in support of Su were detained briefly. Authorities detained Su in 2014 and had held her for more than two years without sentencing her. She was refused a request for medical parole in September. Her husband reported being under police surveillance.

Concerts, sports events, exercise classes, or other meetings of more than 200 persons require approval from public security authorities. Large numbers of public gatherings in Beijing and elsewhere were not revived during the year after being canceled at the last minute or denied government permits in 2015, ostensibly under the guise of ensuring public safety.

Freedom of Association

The constitution provides for freedom of association, but the government restricted this right. CCP policy and government regulations require that all professional, social, and economic organizations officially register with and receive approval from the government. These regulations prevented the formation of autonomous political, human rights, religious, spiritual, labor, and other organizations that the government believed might challenge its authority in any area.

The government maintained tight controls over civil society organizations and in some cases detained or harassed NGO workers.

In January authorities detained a Swedish NGO worker, Peter Dahlin, on charges of endangering state security. He had worked for an organization that trained and supported activists and lawyers seeking to "promote the development of the rule of law." After being paraded on state television in what his friends and colleagues characterized as a forced confession, which included an apology for "hurting the Chinese government and the Chinese people," authorities deported Dahlin from the country.

On April 15, police detained 15 human rights activists while they ate dinner in a restaurant in Guangzhou. The activists had planned to gather at the Guangzhou Municipal Intermediate People's Court the next day to show support for four prominent activists who faced charges of subversion for expressing their support for Hong Kong's 2014 prodemocracy protest movement.

The regulatory system for NGOs was highly restrictive, but specific requirements varied depending on whether an organization was foreign or domestic. Domestic NGOs were governed by the Charity Law, which went into effect in September, and a host of related regulations. Domestic NGOs could register as one of three categories: a social group, a social organization, or a foundation. All domestic NGOs were required to register under the Ministry of Civil Affairs and find an officially sanctioned sponsor to serve as their "professional supervisory unit." Finding a sponsor was often challenging, since the sponsor could be held civilly or criminally responsible for the NGO's activities. All organizations were also required to report their sources of funding, including foreign funding. Domestic NGOs continued to adjust to this new regulatory framework.

On August 22, the CCP Central Committee issued a directive mandating the establishment of CCP cells within all domestic NGOs by 2020. According to authorities, these CCP organizations operating inside domestic NGOs would "strengthen guidance" of NGOs in areas such as "decision making for important projects, important professional activities, major expenditures and funds, acceptance of large donations, and activities involving foreigners." The directive also mandates that authorities conduct annual "spot checks" to ensure compliance on "ideological political work, party building, financial and personnel management, study sessions, foreign exchange, acceptance of foreign donations and assistance, and conducting activities according to their charter." An editorial in the CCP's official mouthpiece, the *People's Daily*, explained how the CCP intends to transform social organizations into CCP affiliates: "Social organizations are important vehicles for the party to connect with and serve the masses; strengthening the party's leadership is the basic guarantee of accelerating the healthy and orderly development of social organizations. We must fully bring into play the combat fortress function of party cells within social organizations."

In April the NPC Standing Committee passed the Law on the Management of Foreign NGOs' Activities within Mainland China (Foreign NGO Management Law), which was scheduled to go into effect in January 2017. The law requires foreign NGOs to register with the Ministry of Public Security and to find a state-sanctioned sponsor for their operations. NGOs that fail to comply face possible civil or criminal penalties. The law provides no appeal process for NGOs denied registration, and it stipulates that NGOs found to have violated certain provisions could be placed on a "blacklist" and barred from operating in the country.

Although the law had not yet gone into effect, some international NGOs reported that it became more difficult to work with local partners, including universities, government agencies, and other domestic NGOs, as the law codified the CCP's perception that foreign NGOs were a "national security" threat. Finding an official sponsor was also difficult for foreign NGOs, as sponsors could be held responsible for the NGO's conduct and had to undertake burdensome reporting requirements. Implementation guidelines and a list of permissible government sponsors were released less than a month before implementation, leaving NGOs uncertain how to comply with the law. Even after a list of sponsors was published, NGOs reported that most government agencies had no unit responsible for sponsoring foreign NGOs. The vague definition of an NGO, as well as of what activities constituted "political" and therefore illegal activities, also left many business organizations and alumni associations uncertain whether they fell under the purview of the law. The lack of clear communication from the government, coupled with harassment by security authorities, caused some foreign NGOs to suspend or cease operations in the country, even before the law took effect.

According to the Ministry of Civil Affairs, by June there were more than 670,000 legally registered social organizations, public institutions, and foundations. According to the Ministry of Public Security, in August there were more than 7,000 foreign NGOs. Many experts believed the actual number of domestic NGOs to be much higher. Domestic NGOs reported that foreign funding dropped during the year, as many domestic NGOs sought to avoid such funding for fear of being labeled as "subversive" in the face of growing restrictions imposed by new laws.

NGOs existed under a variety of formal and informal guises, including national mass organizations created and funded by the CCP that are organizationally prohibited from exercising any independence, known as government-operated NGOs or GONGOs.

For donations to a domestic organization from a foreign NGO, the Foreign NGO Management Law requires foreign NGOs to maintain a representative office in the country in order to send funds or to use the bank account of a domestic NGO when conducting temporary activities. Foreign NGOs are prohibited from using any other method to send and receive funds under the law, and such funding must be reported to the Ministry of Public Security. Foreign NGOs are prohibited from fundraising and "for-profit activities" under the law.

Although all registered organizations came under some degree of government control, some NGOs, primarily service-oriented GONGOs, were able to operate with less day-to-day scrutiny. Authorities supported the growth of some NGOs that focused on social problems, such as poverty alleviation and disaster relief. Law and regulations explicitly prohibited organizations from conducting political or religious activities, and organizations that refused to comply faced criminal penalties.

Authorities continued to restrict and evict local NGOs that received foreign funding and international NGOs that provided assistance to Tibetan communities in the TAR and other Tibetan areas. Almost all were forced to curtail their activities altogether due to travel restrictions, official intimidation of staff members, and the failure of local partners to renew project agreements.

No laws or regulations specifically governed the formation of political parties. The Chinese Democracy Party (CDP) remained banned, and the government continued to monitor, detain, and imprison current and former CDP members. Activists Chen Shuqing and Lu Gengsong, who had been active with the banned CDP, were sentenced to more than 10 years' imprisonment on charges of "subversion of state power" in June.

c. Freedom of Religion

See the Department of State's *International Religious Freedom Report* at www.state.gov/religiousfreedomreport/.

d. Freedom of Movement, Internally Displaced Persons, Protection of Refugees, and Stateless Persons

The law provides for freedom of internal movement, foreign travel, emigration, and repatriation, but the government at times did not respect these rights.

While seriously restricting its scope of operations, the government occasionally cooperated with the Office of the UN High Commissioner for Refugees (UNHCR), which maintained an office in Beijing, to provide protection and assistance to select categories of refugees, asylum seekers, and other persons of concern.

The government increasingly silenced activists by denying them permission to travel, both internationally and domestically, or keeping them under unofficial house arrest.

Abuse of Migrants, Refugees, and Stateless Persons: There were reports that North Korean agents operated clandestinely within the country to forcibly repatriate North Korean citizens. According to press reports, some North Koreans detained by Chinese authorities faced repatriation unless they could pay bribes to secure their release.

In-country Movement: Authorities heightened restrictions on freedom of movement, particularly to curtail the movement of individuals deemed politically sensitive before key anniversaries, visits by foreign dignitaries, or major political events, as well as to forestall demonstrations. Freedom of movement for Tibetans continued to be very limited in the TAR and other Tibetan areas. Public security officers maintained checkpoints in most counties and on roads leading into many towns as well as within major cities, such as Lhasa. Restrictions were not applied to Han Chinese migrants or tourists in Tibetan areas.

Although the government maintained restrictions on the freedom to change one's workplace or residence, the national household registration system (hukou) continued to change, and the ability of most citizens to move within the country to work and live continued to expand. Rural residents continued to migrate to the cities, where the per capita disposable income was approximately three times the rural per capita income, but many could not change their official residence or workplace within the country. Most cities had annual quotas for the number of new temporary residence permits that could be issued, and all workers, including university graduates, had to compete for a limited number of such permits. It was particularly difficult for rural residents to obtain household registration in more economically developed urban areas.

A 2014 State Council legal opinion removed restrictions on rural migrants seeking household registration in small and mid-sized towns and cities. The regulations base household registrations on place of residence and employment instead of place of birth. The opinion exempts cities with large populations.

The household registration system added to the difficulties faced by rural residents, even after they relocated to urban areas and found employment. According to the *Statistical Communique of the People's Republic of China on 2015 National Economic and Social Development* published by the Ministry of Human Resources and Social Security, 294 million persons lived outside the jurisdiction of their household registration. Of that number, 247 million individuals worked outside their home district. Many migrant workers and their families faced numerous obstacles with regard to working conditions and labor rights. Many were unable to access public services, such as public education for their children or social insurance, in the cities where they lived and worked because they were not legally registered urban residents. Poor treatment and difficulty integrating into local communities contributed to increased unrest among migrant workers in the Pearl River Delta. Migrant workers had little recourse when abused by employers and officials. Some major cities maintained programs to provide migrant workers and their children access to public education and other social services free of charge, but migrants in some locations reported difficulty in obtaining these benefits due to onerous bureaucratic processes.

Under the "staying at prison employment" system applicable to recidivists incarcerated in administrative detention, authorities denied certain persons permission to return to their homes after serving their sentences. Some released or paroled prisoners returned home but did not have freedom of movement.

Foreign Travel: The government permitted legal emigration and foreign travel for most citizens. Government employees and retirees, especially from the military, continued to face foreign travel restrictions. The government expanded the use of exit controls for departing passengers at airports and other border crossings to deny foreign travel to some dissidents and persons employed in government posts. Throughout the year many lawyers, artists, authors, and other activists were at times prevented from exiting the country. Authorities also blocked travel of some family members of rights activists.

Border officials and police cited threats to "national security" as the reason for refusing permission to leave the country. Authorities stopped most such persons at the airport at the time of their attempted travel. In January authorities detained journalist Jia Jia at the Beijing airport as he attempted to board a flight to Hong Kong. They held him for nearly two weeks with no charges and interrogated him about an open letter published online calling for Xi Jinping to resign.

Most citizens could obtain passports, although individuals the government deemed potential political threats, including religious leaders, political dissidents, petitioners, and ethnic minorities, routinely reported being refused passports or otherwise prevented from traveling overseas. The passport of former political prisoner and Falun Gong practitioner Wang Zhiwen was physically cancelled at a border checkpoint as he attempted to leave the country.

Uighurs, particularly those residing in the XUAR, reported great difficulty in getting passport applications approved at the local level. They were frequently denied passports to travel abroad, particularly to Saudi Arabia for the Hajj, to other Muslim countries, or to Western countries for academic purposes. Since October authorities ordered residents in some areas of the XUAR to turn in their passports or told residents no new passports were available. The passport recall, however, was not limited to Uighur areas. Family members of Uighur activists living overseas were also denied visas to enter the country.

Uighurs in the XUAR also faced restrictions on movement within the XUAR itself. Although the use of "domestic passports" that called for local official approval before traveling to another area was discontinued in May, identification checks remained in place when entering cities and on public roads. Reuters reported that authorities required applicants for travel documents to provide extra information prior to the month of Ramadan. For example, residents in the Ili Kazakh Autonomous Prefecture in the XUAR had to provide DNA samples, fingerprints, and voice recordings in order to apply for travel documents, according a local government newspaper in June.

In the TAR and Tibetan areas of Qinghai, Gansu, Yunnan, and Sichuan Provinces, Tibetans, especially Buddhist monks and nuns, experienced great difficulty acquiring passports. The unwillingness of Chinese authorities in Tibetan areas to issue or renew passports for Tibetans created, in effect, a ban on foreign travel for a large segment of the Tibetan population. Han Chinese residents of Tibetan areas did not experience the same difficulties.

<u>Exile</u>: The law neither provides for a citizen's right to repatriate nor addresses exile. The government continued to refuse re-entry to numerous citizens considered dissidents, Falun Gong activists, or "troublemakers." Although authorities allowed some dissidents living abroad to return, dissidents released on medical parole and allowed to leave the country often were effectively exiled.

<u>Emigration and Repatriation</u>: The government continued to try to prevent many Tibetans and Uighurs from leaving the country and detained many who were apprehended while attempting to leave (see Tibet Annex). Some family members of rights activists who tried to emigrate were unable to do so.

Protection of Refugees

<u>Access to Asylum</u>: The law does not provide for the granting of refugee or asylee status. The government did not have a system for providing protection to refugees but allowed UNHCR to assist the relatively small number of non-North Korean and non-Burmese refugees. The government did not officially recognize these individuals as refugees; they remained in the country as illegal immigrants unable to work, with no access to education, and subject to deportation at any time.

Authorities continued to repatriate North Korean refugees forcibly, including trafficking victims, generally treating them as illegal economic migrants. The government detained and deported such refugees to North Korea, where they faced severe punishment or death, including in North Korean forced-labor camps. The government did not provide North Korean trafficking victims with legal alternatives to repatriation. The government continued to prevent UNHCR from having access to North Korean or Burmese refugees. Authorities sometimes detained and prosecuted citizens who assisted North Korean refugees as well as those who facilitated illegal border crossings.

In some instances the government pressured neighboring countries to return asylum seekers or UNHCR-recognized refugees to China. At year's end India was reportedly preparing to return to China two Uighur asylum seekers who had been convicted of crimes in India.

<u>Refoulement</u>: The government did not provide protection against the expulsion or forcible return of vulnerable refugees and asylum seekers, especially North Korean refugees. The government continued to consider North Koreans as "illegal economic migrants" rather than refugees or asylum seekers and forcibly returned

many of them to North Korea. The government continued to deny UNHCR permission to operate outside of Beijing.

Access to Basic Services: North Korean asylum seekers and North Koreans in the country seeking economic opportunities generally did not have access to health care, public education, or other social services due to lack of legal status. International media reported that as many as 30,000 children born to North Korean women in China, most of whom were married to Chinese spouses, were denied access to public services, including education and health care, despite provisions in the law that provide citizenship to children with at least one PRC citizen parent.

Durable Solutions: The government largely cooperated with UNHCR when dealing with the resettlement in China of Han Chinese or ethnic minorities from Vietnam and Laos living in the country since the Vietnam War era. The government and UNHCR continued discussions concerning the granting of citizenship to these long-term residents and their children, many of whom were born in China. The government worked with UNHCR in granting exit permission for a small number of non-Burmese and non-North Korean refugees to resettle to third countries.

Section 3. Freedom to Participate in the Political Process

The constitution states that "all power in the People's Republic of China belongs to the people" and that the organs through which the people exercise state power are the NPC and the people's congresses at provincial, district, and local levels. In practice the CCP dictated the legislative agenda to the NPC. While the law provides for elections of people's congress delegates at the county level and below, citizens could not freely choose the officials who governed them. The CCP controlled all elections and continued to control appointments to positions of political power. The CCP used various intimidation tactics, including house arrest, to block independent candidates from standing for local elections.

Elections and Political Participation

Recent Elections: In 2013 the NPC's nearly 3,000 delegates elected the president and vice president, the premier and vice premiers, and the chairman of the Central Military Commission. The NPC Standing Committee, which consisted of 175 members, oversaw the elections and determined the agenda and procedures for the NPC. The selection of NPC members takes place every five years, and the process is controlled by the CCP.

The NPC Standing Committee remained under the direct authority of the CCP, and all important legislative decisions required the concurrence of the CCP's seven-member Politburo Standing Committee. Despite its broad authority under the state constitution, the NPC did not set policy independently or remove political leaders without the CCP's approval.

According to Ministry of Civil Affairs' statistics, almost all of the country's more than 600,000 villages had implemented direct elections for members of local subgovernmental organizations known as village committees. The direct election of officials by ordinary citizens remained narrow in scope and strictly confined to the lowest rungs of local governance. Corruption, vote buying, and interference by township-level and CCP officials continued to be problems. The law permits each voter to cast proxy votes for up to three other voters.

The election law governs legislative bodies at all levels, although compliance and enforcement varied across the country. Under the law citizens have the opportunity every five years to vote for local people's congress representatives at the county level and below, although in most cases higher-level government officials or CCP cadres controlled the nomination of candidates. At higher levels legislators selected people's congress delegates from among their ranks. For example, provincial-level people's congresses selected delegates to the NPC. Local CCP secretaries generally served concurrently within the leadership team of the local people's congress, thus strengthening CCP control over legislatures.

In September the NPC Standing Committee expelled 45 deputies from Liaoning Province for violations of the electoral law, including vote buying and bribery. Official media described the case as "unprecedented since the founding of the People's Republic of China in 1949." More than 500 of the 617 members of the Liaoning Provincial People's Congress were implicated in the scandal and either resigned or were expelled from the body. The NPC Standing Committee also disbanded the Liaoning Provincial People's Congress Standing Committee and established a preparatory panel to function on its behalf until convening of a new provincial people's congress.

<u>Political Parties and Political Participation</u>: Official statements asserted that "the political party system [that] China has adopted is multiparty cooperation and political consultation" under CCP leadership. The CCP, however, retained a monopoly on political power, and the government forbade the creation of new political parties. The government officially recognized nine parties founded prior

to 1949, and parties other than the CCP held 30 percent of the seats in the NPC. These non-CCP members did not function as a political opposition. They exercised very little influence on legislation or policymaking and were allowed to operate only under the direction of the CCP United Front Work Department.

No laws or regulations specifically govern the formation of political parties. The Chinese Democracy Party (CDP) remained banned, and the government continued to monitor, detain, and imprison current and former CDP members. Activists attempting to create or support unofficial parties were arrested, detained, or confined.

Participation of Women and Minorities: While the government placed no special restrictions on the participation of women or minority groups in the political process, women held few positions of significant influence in the government or CCP structure. Among the 2,987 appointed delegates to the 12th NPC in 2013, 699 (23 percent) were women. Following the 18th CCP Congress in 2013, two women were members of the CCP Central Committee's 25-member Politburo. There were no women in the Politburo Standing Committee.

The election law provides a general mandate for quotas for female and ethnic minority representatives, but achieving these quotas often required election authorities to violate the election law.

A total of 409 delegates from 55 ethnic minorities were members of the 12th NPC, accounting for 14 percent of the total number of delegates. All of the country's officially recognized minority groups were represented. The 18th Communist Party Congress in 2013 elected 10 members of ethnic minority groups as members of the 205-person Central Committee. There was no ethnic minority member of the Politburo and only one ethnic minority was serving as a party secretary of a provincial-level jurisdiction, although a handful of ethnic minority members were serving as leaders in provincial governments. In March an ethnic Mongolian woman, Bu Xiaolin, became chair of the Inner Mongolia Autonomous Region, equivalent to a provincial governor. In July an ethnic Hui woman, Xian Hui, also became chair of the Ningxia Hui Autonomous Region.

Section 4. Corruption and Lack of Transparency in Government

Although officials faced criminal penalties for corruption, the government and the CCP did not implement the law consistently or transparently. Corruption remained rampant, and many cases of corruption involved areas heavily regulated by the government, such as land-usage rights, real estate, mining, and infrastructure development, which were susceptible to fraud, bribery, and kickbacks. Court judgments often could not be enforced against powerful special entities, including government departments, state-owned enterprises, military personnel, and some members of the CCP.

In January the Central Commission for Discipline Inspection (CCDI), the CCP's investigative body that enforces political discipline among its members, including countering corruption, reported that in 2015 it received more than 2.8 million allegations of corruption, investigated 330,000 corruption-related cases, and disciplined 336,000 officials, 44 percent more than in 2014. Among those investigated, 42 senior officials at the vice-ministerial level or above in the CCP, government, and state-owned enterprises were eventually removed from their posts. In addition, 34,000 officials were punished for violating one or more of the "eight rules" that serve as the mandate for the anticorruption campaign, 52 percent less than 2014. The CCDI continued to operate outside the judicial system, and in many cases it punished CCP members and officials in the absence of a judicial process.

The CCP internal disciplinary system used to investigate party members suspected of corruption and other violations of party rules--known as "shuanggui"--continued to operate without legal oversight and with widespread allegations of torture. Many officials accused of corruption or other discipline violations were interrogated and in some cases tortured while under investigation by the CCP, often to extract a confession of wrongdoing. Some were later turned over to the judicial system for criminal prosecution.

Corruption: In numerous cases public officials and leaders of state-owned enterprises, who generally held high CCP ranks, were investigated for corruption. In March, Procurator General Cao Jianming reported to the 12th NPC that in 2015 the government investigated 4,568 public servants above the county level for corruption, including 41 at the provincial and ministerial levels or above, in 4,490 cases of graft, bribery, and embezzlement of public funds, each involving more than one million yuan ($145,000). While the tightly controlled state media apparatus publicized some notable corruption investigations, as a general matter, there were very few details regarding the process by which CCP and government officials were investigated for corruption.

In January the CCP announced it was investigating National Bureau of Statistics head Wang Bao'an. Wang was expelled from the CCP in August for accepting bribes, and his case was turned over to judicial officials for prosecution.

In March the CCP announced it was investigating former Liaoning provincial CCP secretary Wang Min. Wang was expelled from the party in August for his association with a bribery and vote-buying scheme involving members of the Liaoning Provincial People's Congress and Liaoning deputies to the NPC.

On July 4, a court sentenced Ling Jihua, a former member of the Politburo and head of the CCP General Office, to life in prison for extorting 77.1 million yuan ($11.2 million), abuse of power, and illegally obtaining state secrets. Ling was one of former president Hu Jintao's closest advisors.

In some cases individuals who tried to report corruption faced reprisal and retribution. In July a real estate developer in Hunan Province, Wu Zhengge, was arrested after he hired a private investigator to find evidence of corruption by several local judges. The judges were presiding over a criminal case against Wu, who hoped to use the evidence to blackmail the judges into dismissing the case. Although the judges were placed under investigation for public corruption, Wu was later arrested and charged with disclosing personal information.

Financial Disclosure: A regulation requires officials in government agencies or state-owned enterprises at the county level or above to report their ownership of property, including that in their spouse's or children's names, as well as their families' investments in financial assets and enterprises. The regulations do not require that declarations be made public. Instead, they are submitted to a higher administrative level and a human resource department. Punishments for not declaring information vary from training on the regulations, warning talks, and adjusting one's work position to being relieved of one's position. Regulations further state that officials should report all income, including allowances, subsidies, and bonuses as well as income from other jobs, such as giving lectures, writing, consulting, reviewing articles, painting, and calligraphy. Officials, their spouses, and the children who live with them also should report their real estate properties and financial investments, although these reports are not made public. They must report whether their children live abroad as well as the work status of their children and grandchildren (including those who live abroad). Officials are required to file reports annually and must report changes of personal status within 30 days.

<u>Public Access to Information</u>: Open-government information regulations allow citizens to request information from the government. The regulations require government authorities to create formal channels for information requests and to include an appeals process if requests are rejected or not answered. They stipulate that administrative agencies should reply to requests immediately to the extent possible. Otherwise, the administrative agency should provide the information within 15 working days, with the possibility of a maximum extension of an additional 15 days. According to the regulations, administrative agencies may collect only cost-based fees (as determined by the State Council) for searching, photocopying, postage, and similar expenses when disclosing government information on request. The regulations include exceptions for state secrets, commercial secrets, and individual privacy.

Publicly released provincial- and national-level statistics for open-government information requests showed wide disparities across localities, levels of government, and departments regarding the number of requests filed and official documents released in response.

If information requesters believed that an administrative agency violated the regulations, they could report it to the next higher-level administrative agency, the supervision agency, or the department in charge of open-government information.

Section 5. Governmental Attitude Regarding International and Nongovernmental Investigation of Alleged Violations of Human Rights

The government sought to maintain control over civil society groups, halt the emergence of independent NGOs, and hinder the activities of civil society and rights' activist groups. The government harassed independent domestic NGOs and did not permit them to openly monitor or comment on human rights conditions. The government made statements expressing suspicion of independent organizations and closely scrutinized NGOs with financial and other links overseas. The government took significant steps during the year to bring all domestic NGOs under its direct regulatory control, thereby curtailing the space for independent NGOs to exist. Most large NGOs were quasi-governmental, and government agencies had to sponsor all official NGOs.

<u>The United Nations or Other International Bodies</u>: In August the UN special rapporteur on extreme poverty and human rights, Philip Alston, visited the country. Alston said that the government restricted his activities and that security agents followed him throughout his visit. Many of his meeting requests were declined,

and although he submitted a list of academics he wanted to meet prior to his visit, he was told that many of them had been advised they should be on vacation during his visit. Security agents detained one person en route to a meeting with Alston. Alston's request to visit was first made in 2005, according to the UN Office of the Human Rights Commissioner. A dozen other requests for visits to the country by UN experts remained outstanding.

The government remained reluctant to accept criticism of its human rights record by other nations or international organizations. It criticized reports by international human rights monitoring groups, claiming that such reports were inaccurate and interfered in the country's internal affairs.

Government Human Rights Bodies: The government maintained that each country's economic, social, cultural, and historical conditions determined its approach to human rights. The government claimed that its treatment of suspects, considered to be victims of human rights abuses by the international community, was in accordance with national law. The government did not have a human rights ombudsman or commission.

Section 6. Discrimination, Societal Abuses, and Trafficking in Persons

Women

Rape and Domestic Violence: Rape is illegal, and some persons convicted of rape were executed. The penalties for rape range from three years in prison to death. The law does not address spousal rape.

Cases of rape were unreported, and most cases were closed through private settlement. From 2013 to 2015, courts adjudicated 66,736 rape cases in which 62,551 defendants were given criminal convictions. Scholars pointed out that performance indicators for public security officers and prosecutors disincentivized prosecution of rape cases, as private settlement of cases minimized the risk that the records of prosecutors and public security officials would be tarnished by mishandled cases. The government, however, acknowledged the need to include the reporting of rape, domestic violence, sexual harassment, and other gender-related cases in annual judicial statistics.

Domestic violence remained a significant problem, but the government took a significant step to protect women from domestic abuse through the passage of the Family Violence Law, which took effect March 1. The law defines domestic violence as physical and mental violence between family members. NGOs reported that, as a result of the law, more women were willing to report domestic violence incidents to police. Nevertheless, implementation of the law remained inconsistent during its first year, largely due to authorities' lack of awareness of the law's implementing measures. Societal sentiment that domestic violence was a personal, private matter also contributed to underreporting and inaction by authorities when women faced violence at home.

According to reports, at least one-quarter of families suffered from domestic violence and more than 85 percent of the victims were women. The government supported shelters for victims of domestic violence, and some courts provided protections to victims, including through restraining orders prohibiting a perpetrator of domestic violence from coming near a victim. Nonetheless, official assistance did not always reach victims, and public security forces often ignored domestic violence. Legal aid institutions working to provide counseling and defense to victims of domestic violence were often pressured to suspend public activities and cease all forms of policy advocacy, an area that was reserved only for government-sponsored organizations. During the year several domestic violence service-oriented organizations were unable to register formally as nonprofit organizations, as authorities rejected their applications.

While domestic violence tended to be more prevalent in rural areas, it also occurred among the highly educated urban population. Women in rural areas, however, often lacked access to protection due to the perception that domestic violence was a lesser crime. In one case in Henan Province, a man was sentenced to death with a two-year reprieve--instead of immediate execution--after murdering his wife. In its written judgement, the court cited the fact that the murder was a "domestic case" in its reasoning for a reduced penalty.

During the year the government began to open dedicated shelters for domestic violence survivors, a change from previous years when survivors could only go to homeless shelters providing domestic violence-related services. Such shelters opened in Chengdu, Dazhou, Nanjing, and Zhengzhou municipalities, offering psychological counseling for victims of domestic abuse, including women and children. The shelters reported they were underutilized due to the public shame associated with domestic violence.

According to women's rights activists, a recurring problem in the prosecution of domestic violence cases was a lack of evidence--including photographs, hospital records, police records, or children's testimony--which hindered their prosecution. Witnesses seldom testified in court.

Courts' recognition of domestic violence improved, making spousal abuse a mitigating factor in crimes committed in self-defense. In 2015 the SPC issued guidelines for dealing with cases of domestic violence to improve the unified application of laws, according to the Information Office of the State Council.

Sexual Harassment: The law bans sexual harassment. Offenders are subject to a penalty of up to 15 days in detention, according to the Beijing Public Security Bureau. Nonetheless, because laws lacked a clear definition of sexual harassment, it remained difficult for victims to file a sexual harassment complaint and for judges to reach a ruling on such cases.

Many women remained unwilling to report incidents of sexual harassment, believing that the justice system was ineffectual, according to official media. Several prominent media reports of sexual harassment went viral on social media, helping to raise awareness of the problem, particularly in the workplace.

The Law on the Protection of Women's Rights and Interests empowers victims to file a sexual harassment complaint with their employer and/or with authorities. If employers failed to take effective measures to prevent sexual harassment, they could be fined.

Sexual harassment was not limited to the workplace. According to a 2014 survey by the All China Women's Federation (ACWF), 57 percent of female students at 15 universities reported having been sexually harassed. Some of them experienced such harassment repeatedly. Many students said they were unaware of formal procedures to report incidents of harassments. At Beijing Normal University, one student documented 60 instances of sexual harassment over the past decade, prompting online debate and the university to start an antiharassment awareness campaign.

The ACWF and universities worked to improve awareness on sexual harassment by offering seminars and classes; however, NGOs that sought to increase public awareness of sexual harassment came under increasing scrutiny. Some women's NGOs reported harassment by public security and faced challenges executing their programs. In September women's rights activist Shan Lihua was found guilty by the Gangzha District People's Court in Nantong, Jiangsu Province, of "picking quarrels and stirring up trouble." The indictment specifically cited Shan's activism on a rape case in Hainan Province as evidence, according to media reports.

Reproductive Rights: On January 1, the government raised the birth limit imposed on its citizens from one to two children per married couple, thereby ending the "one-child policy" first enacted in 1979. The revised law permits married couples to have two children and allows couples to apply for permission to have a third child if they meet conditions stipulated in local and provincial regulations. The revised law did not, however, eliminate state-imposed birth limitations or the penalties that citizens face for violating the law. The government considers intrauterine devices (IUDs) and sterilization to be the most reliable form of birth control and compelled women to accept the insertion of IUDs by officials. The National Health and Family Planning Commission reported that all provinces eliminated an earlier requirement to seek approval for a birth before a first child was conceived, but provinces could still require parents to "register pregnancies" prior to giving birth, which could be used as a de facto permit system in some provinces.

Under the law and in practice, there continued to be financial and administrative penalties for births that exceed birth limits or otherwise violate regulations. The National Health and Family Planning Commission announced it would continue to impose fines, called "social compensation fees," for policy violations. The law as implemented requires each woman with an unauthorized pregnancy to abort or pay the social compensation fee, which can reach 10 times a person's annual disposable income. The exact level of the fee varied widely from province to province. Those with financial means often paid the fee so that their children born in violation of the birth restrictions would have access to services. Some parents avoided the fee by hiding a child born in violation of the law with friends or relatives.

The revised law maintains previous language indicating that "citizens have an obligation to practice birth planning in accordance with the law" and also states that "couples of child-bearing age voluntarily choose birth planning contraceptive and birth control measures to prevent and reduce unwanted pregnancies." Regulations pertaining to single women and unmarried couples remain unchanged. Children born to single mothers or unmarried couples are considered "outside of the policy" and subject to the social compensation fee and the denial of legal documents, such as birth documents and the "hukou" residence permit. Single women can avoid those penalties by marrying within 60 days of the baby's birth.

In localities with large populations of migrant workers, officials specifically targeted migrant women to ensure that they did not exceed birth limitations.

Government statistics on the percentage of abortions during the year that were nonelective were not available. State media claimed the number of coerced abortions had declined in recent years in the wake of looser regulations, including the implementation of the two-child policy.

As in prior years, population control policy continued to rely on social pressure, education, propaganda, and economic penalties as well as on measures such as mandatory pregnancy examinations and coercive abortions and sterilizations. Those found to have a pregnancy in violation of the law or those who helped another to evade state controls could face punitive measures, such as onerous fines, job loss, demotion, and loss of promotion opportunity (for those in the public sector or state-owned enterprises), expulsion from the CCP (membership is an unofficial requirement for many jobs), and other administrative punishments. In July the state-funded news outlet *Sixth Tone* reported that officials in Guangdong Province threatened a remarried couple with termination of their employment unless the wife had an abortion. Both individuals were government employees and each had a child from a prior marriage. Regulations in Guangdong Province do not permit such couples to have a child.

Regulations requiring women who violate the family-planning policy to terminate their pregnancies still exist and were enforced in some provinces, such as Hubei, Hunan, and Liaoning. For example, Hunan provincial regulations that were revised in March stipulate: "Pregnancies that do not conform to the conditions established by the law should promptly be terminated. For those who have not promptly terminated the pregnancy, the township people's government or subdistrict office shall order that the pregnancy be terminated by a deadline." Other provinces, such as Jilin, removed previous requirements to terminate pregnancies that violate the policy but retained provisions that require local officials to "promptly report" to higher authorities when such pregnancies are discovered without specifying what measures will be taken thereafter. Other provinces, such as Guizhou, Jiangxi, Qinghai, and Yunnan, maintained provisions that require "remedial measures," an official euphemism for abortion, to deal with pregnancies that violate the policy. Some provinces, such as Guangdong, removed provisions from provincial-level regulations requiring "remedial measures" but inserted them instead into the revised regulations of major municipalities, such as Shenzhen. In the provinces where provincial regulations do not explicitly require termination of pregnancy or remedial measures, some local officials still coerced abortions to avoid surpassing population growth quotas.

The law mandates that family planning bureaus administer pregnancy tests to married women of childbearing age and provide them with unspecified "follow-up" services. Some provinces fined women who did not undergo these periodic state-mandated pregnancy tests. Officials at all levels could receive rewards or penalties based on whether or not they met the population targets set by their administrative region. Promotions for local officials depended in part on meeting population targets.

Although the population and birth planning law states that officials should not violate citizens' "lawful rights" in the enforcement of birth limitation policy, these rights are not clearly defined nor are the penalties for violating them. The law lists seven activities that authorities are prohibited from undertaking when enforcing birth control regulations, which include beating individuals and their families, destroying property or crops, confiscating property to cover the amount of the fee, detaining relatives, and conducting pregnancy tests on unmarried women. Forced abortion is not listed. By law citizens may sue officials who exceed their authority in implementing birth-planning policy, but few protections exist for citizens against retaliation from local officials.

Discrimination: The constitution states that "women enjoy equal rights with men in all spheres of life." The law provides for equality in ownership of property, inheritance rights, access to education, and equal pay for equal work. Despite this, many activists and observers expressed concern that discrimination remained a problem. Women reported that discrimination, unfair dismissal, demotion, and wage discrepancies were significant problems.

On average, women earned 35 percent less than men doing similar work. This wage gap was greater in rural areas. Women also continued to be underrepresented in leadership positions, despite their high rate of participation in the labor force. In 2015 women constituted 17 percent of legislators, senior officials, and managers.

Authorities often did not enforce laws protecting the rights of women. According to legal experts, it was difficult to litigate sex discrimination suits because of vague legal definitions. Some observers noted that the agencies tasked with protecting women's rights tended to focus on maternity-related benefits and wrongful termination during maternity leave rather than on sex discrimination, violence against women, and sexual harassment.

In April a Guangzhou court sided with a female plaintiff, Gao Xiao, who had sued a restaurant for refusing to hire her as a cook after she was told the job was only open to men. The court ordered that Gao be paid 2,000 yuan ($290) in compensation. This was reportedly Guangzhou's first gender-discrimination lawsuit.

Women's rights advocates indicated that in rural areas women often forfeited land and property rights to their husbands in divorce proceedings. Rural contract law and laws protecting women's rights stipulate that women enjoy equal rights in cases of land management, but experts asserted that this was rarely the case due to the complexity of the law and difficulties in its implementation.

Gender-biased Sex Selection: According to the National Bureau of Statistics of China, the sex ratio at birth was 113 males to 100 females in 2016, a decline from 2013, when the ratio was 116 males for every 100 females. Sex identification and sex-selective abortion are prohibited, but the practices continued because of traditional preference for male children and the birth-limitation policy.

Children

Birth Registration: Citizenship is derived from parents. Parents must register their children in compliance with the national household registration system within one month of birth. Unregistered children could not access public services, including education. No data was available on the number of unregistered births. In 2010 the official census estimated there were 13 million individuals without official documentation, many of whom likely were "ghost" children whose births were concealed from local officials because they violated the population control policy. Some local officials denied such children household registration and identification documents, particularly if their families could not pay the social compensation fees.

Education: Although the law provides for nine years of compulsory education for children, many children did not attend school for the required period in economically disadvantaged rural areas, and some never attended. Although public schools were not allowed to charge tuition, many schools continued to charge miscellaneous fees because they received insufficient local and central government funding. Such fees and other school-related expenses made it difficult for poorer families and some migrant workers to send their children to school.

Denied access to state-run schools, most children of migrant workers who attended school did so at unlicensed and poorly equipped schools.

Child Abuse: The physical abuse of children is ground for criminal prosecution. Kidnapping, buying, and selling children for adoption existed, particularly in poor rural areas, but there were no reliable estimates of the number of children kidnapped. Government authorities regularly estimated that fewer than 10,000 children were abducted per year, but media reports and experts sources noted that as many as 70,000 may be kidnapped every year. Most children kidnapped internally were sold to couples unable to have children. Those convicted of buying an abducted child could be sentenced to three years' imprisonment. In the past most children abducted were boys, but increased demand for children reportedly drove kidnappers to focus on girls as well. In an effort to reunite families, the Ministry of Public Security maintained a DNA database of parents of missing children and of children recovered in law enforcement operations. During the year the government adopted a telephone system similar to the Amber Alert system in the United States.

Between 2013 and 2015, courts adjudicated 7,610 child molestation cases, sentencing 6,620 individuals. The number of convictions in child molestation cases consistently increased between 2013 and 2015. In a report during the year, the SPC acknowledged there had been a high number of cases involving the sexual abuse of minors. The People's Public Security University of China estimated that, for every reported case of sexual abuse, as many as seven cases went unreported.

Early and Forced Marriage: The legal minimum age for marriage is 22 for men and 20 for women. Child marriage was not known to be a problem.

Sexual Exploitation of Children: Persons who forced girls under the age of 14 into prostitution could be sentenced to seven years to life in prison in addition to a fine or confiscation of property. In especially serious cases, violators could receive a life sentence or death sentence, in addition to having their property confiscated. Those who visited girls forced into prostitution under age 14 were subject to five years or more in prison in addition to paying a fine.

The minimum legal age for consensual sex is 14.

Pornography of any kind, including child pornography, is illegal. Under the criminal code, those producing, reproducing, publishing, selling, or disseminating obscene materials with the purpose of making a profit could be sentenced up to three years in prison or put under criminal detention or surveillance in addition to paying a fine. Offenders in serious cases could receive prison sentences of three to 10 years in addition to paying a fine.

Persons broadcasting or showing obscene materials to minors under the age of 18 are to be "severely punished."

Infanticide or Infanticide of Children with Disabilities: The law forbids infanticide, but there was evidence that the practice continued. According to the National Health and Family Planning Commission, at least one doctor was charged with infanticide. No other statistics on the practice were available. Female infanticide, gender-biased abortions, and the abandonment and neglect of baby girls were declining but continued to be a problem in some circumstances due to the traditional preference for sons and the birth-limitation policy.

Displaced Children: There were approximately 1.5 million street children, according to the UN Development Program. There were between 150,000 and one million urban street children, according to state media. This number could be even higher if the children of migrant workers who spent the day on the streets were included. In 2013 the ACWF estimated that more than 61 million children under the age of 17 were left behind by their migrant-worker parents in rural areas.

Institutionalized Children: The law forbids the mistreatment or abandonment of children. The vast majority of children in orphanages were girls, many of whom were abandoned. Boys in orphanages usually had disabilities or were in poor health. Medical professionals sometimes advised parents of children with disabilities to put the children into orphanages.

The government denied that children in orphanages were mistreated or refused medical care but acknowledged that the system often was unable to provide adequately for some children, particularly those with serious medical problems. Adopted children were counted under the birth-limitation regulations in most locations. As a result, couples who adopted abandoned infant girls were sometimes barred from having additional children. The law was changed during the year to allow children who are rescued to be made available for adoption within one year if their family is not identified.

International Child Abductions: The country is not a party to the 1980 Hague Convention on the Civil Aspects of International Child Abduction. See the

Department of State's *Annual Report on International Parental Child Abduction* at travel.state.gov/content/childabduction/en/legal/compliance.html.

Anti-Semitism

The government does not recognize Judaism as an ethnicity or religion. According to information from the Jewish Virtual Library, the country's Jewish population was 2,500 in 2014. In September the *New York Times* reported that members of the Kaifeng Jewish community in Henan Province came under pressure from authorities. Approximately 1,000 Kaifeng citizens claimed Jewish ancestry. Media reports stated that authorities forced the only Jewish learning center in the community to shut down.

Trafficking in Persons

See the Department of State's *Trafficking in Persons Report* at www.state.gov/j/tip/rls/tiprpt/.

Persons with Disabilities

The law protects the rights of persons with disabilities and prohibits discrimination, but in many instances conditions for such persons lagged behind legal requirements and failed to provide persons with disabilities access to programs intended to assist them. The Ministry of Civil Affairs and the China Disabled Persons Federation (CDPF), a government-organized civil association, are the main entities responsible for persons with disabilities.

According to the law, persons with disabilities "are entitled to enjoyment of equal rights as other citizens in political, economic, cultural, and social fields, in family life, and in other aspects." Discrimination against, insult of, and infringement upon persons with disabilities is prohibited. The law prohibits discrimination against minors with disabilities and codifies a variety of judicial protections for juveniles.

Publicly available statistics showed conflicting information about the education rate for children with disabilities. The Ministry of Education reported that there were more than 2,000 special education schools for children with disabilities and that 83,000 children remained outside the state education system, mostly in rural areas. In August the CDPF reported that more than 140,000 school-age children with disabilities were in need of suitable education. NGOs reported that only 2 percent of the 20 million children with disabilities had access to education that met their needs.

Individuals with disabilities faced difficulties accessing higher education. The law permits universities to exclude candidates with disabilities who would otherwise be qualified. In 2015, of the country's 7.4 million college freshman, only 8,508 had disabilities. A regulation mandates accommodations for students with disabilities when taking the national university entrance exam.

Nearly 100,000 organizations existed, mostly in urban areas, to serve those with disabilities and protect their legal rights. The government, at times in conjunction with NGOs, sponsored programs to integrate persons with disabilities into society.

Misdiagnosis, inadequate medical care, stigmatization, and abandonment remained common problems. Parents who chose to keep children with disabilities at home generally faced difficulty finding adequate medical care, day care, and education for their children. Government statistics reported that four million persons with disabilities lived in poverty.

Unemployment among adults with disabilities, in part due to discrimination, remained a serious problem. In April the Ministry of Human Resources and Social Security reported that, of the country's 85 million reported persons with disabilities, 4.3 million were employed in urban areas and 16.7 million were employed in rural areas. The law requires local governments to offer incentives to enterprises that hire persons with disabilities. Regulations in some parts of the country also require employers to pay into a national fund for persons with disabilities when employees with disabilities do not make up a statutory minimum percentage of the total workforce. In some parts of the country, billboard advertisements informed companies that they needed to pay a disability "tax" rather than encouraging them to hire persons with disabilities. In some cases otherwise qualified candidates were denied jobs because of physical disabilities. In August the government reported that at least four million persons with disabilities lived in poverty.

Standards adopted for making roads and buildings accessible to persons with disabilities are subject to the Law on the Handicapped, which calls for their "gradual" implementation. Compliance with the law was limited.

The law forbids the marriage of persons with certain mental disabilities, such as schizophrenia. If doctors found that a couple was at risk of transmitting congenital disabilities to their children, the couple could marry only if they agree to use birth control or undergo sterilization. In some instances officials continued to require couples to abort pregnancies when doctors discovered possible disabilities during prenatal examinations. The law stipulates that local governments must employ such practices to raise the percentage of births of children without disabilities.

National/Racial/Ethnic Minorities

Most minority groups resided in areas they had traditionally inhabited. Government policy called for members of recognized minorities to receive preferential treatment in birth planning, university admission, access to loans, and employment. The substance and implementation of ethnic minority policies nonetheless remained poor, and discrimination against minorities remained widespread.

Minority groups in border and other regions had less access to education than their Han Chinese counterparts, faced job discrimination in favor of Han Chinese migrants, and earned incomes well below those in other parts of the country. Government development programs often disrupted traditional living patterns of minority groups and in some cases included the forced relocation of persons and the forced settlement of nomads. Han Chinese benefited disproportionately from government programs and economic growth in minority areas. Some job advertisements in the XUAR made clear that Uighur applicants would not be considered for employment. As part of its emphasis on building a "harmonious society" and maintaining social stability, the government downplayed racism and institutional discrimination against minorities, which remained the source of deep resentment in the XUAR, the Inner Mongolia Autonomous Region, the TAR, and other Tibetan areas.

Ethnic minorities represented approximately 13.7 percent of delegates to the NPC and more than 15 percent of NPC Standing Committee members, according to an official report issued in 2014. Han Chinese officials continued to hold the majority of the most powerful CCP and government positions in minority autonomous regions, particularly the XUAR.

The government's policy to encourage Han Chinese migration into minority areas significantly increased the population of Han in the XUAR. In recent decades, the Chinese-Uighur ratio in the capital of Urumqi reversed from 20/80 to approximately 80/20 and continued to be a source of Uighur resentment. Discriminatory hiring practices gave preference to Han Chinese and reduced job prospects for ethnic minorities. Arable land in the XUAR's Hotan Prefecture was appropriated from Uighur residents and distributed to Han Chinese migrants, Radio Free Asia reported in April.

According to a November 2015 government census, 9.5 million, or 40 percent, of the XUAR's official residents were Han Chinese. Uighur, Hui, Kazakh, Kyrgyz, and other ethnic minorities constituted 14.1 million XUAR residents, or 60 percent of the total population. Official statistics understated the Han Chinese population because they did not count the more than 2.7 million Han residents on paramilitary compounds (bingtuan) and those who were long-term "temporary workers," an increase of 1.2 percent over the previous year, according to a 2015 government of Xinjiang report. As the government continued to promote Han migration into the XUAR and filled local jobs with domestic migrant labor, local officials coerced young Uighur men and women to participate in a government-sponsored labor transfer program to cities outside the XUAR, according to overseas human rights organizations. In April, Radio Free Asia reported that local authorities in Hotan Prefecture ordered Uighur men and women to take part in a labor program to prevent their involvement in "illegal activities" and promote stability in the area.

The law states that "schools (classes and grades) and other institutions of education where most of the students come from minority nationalities shall, whenever possible, use textbooks in their own languages and use their languages as the medium of instruction." Despite guarantees of cultural and linguistic rights, many primary, middle, and high school students in the XUAR had limited access to Uighur-language instruction and textbooks. There were reports that private Uighur-language schools were shut by authorities without any transparent investigation under the pretense that they promoted radical ideologies. Uighur students were often provided insufficient Uighur-language resources and instruction to maintain the integrity of their culture and traditions.

Officials in the XUAR continued to implement a pledge to crack down on the government-designated "three evil forces" of religious extremism, ethnic separatism, and violent terrorism, and they outlined efforts to launch a concentrated re-education campaign to combat what it deems to be separatism. The government in December 2015 adopted a counterterrorism law defining terrorism broadly in a way that could include religious, political, and ethnic expression. In August the XUAR government adopted a provincial-level interpretation of the national legislation, expanding the definition of terrorism to include the use of cell phones to spread terrorist ideology and "twisting" the concept of halal to apply to nonfood aspects of life. Some security raids, arbitrary detentions, and judicial punishments, ostensibly directed at individuals or organizations suspected of promoting the "three evil forces," appeared to target groups or individuals peacefully seeking to express their political or religious views. Officials continued to use the threat of violence as justification for extreme security measures directed at the local population, journalists, and visiting foreigners.

Uighurs continued to be sentenced to long prison terms and in some cases executed without due process on charges of separatism and endangering state security. Economist Ilham Tohti remained in prison, where he was serving a life sentence, after being convicted on separatist-related charges in 2014. Many governments continued to call for his release, and Tohti was awarded the Martin Ennals Foundation's human rights award.

In January, Xinjiang-based activist Zhang Haitao was sentenced to 19 years in prison on charges of "inciting subversion of state power" and "probing and supplying intelligence abroad." Haitao, who is Han Chinese, had been publicly critical of the government's policies toward Uighurs. In November a Xinjiang court upheld the sentence.

Authorities detained Uighur social activists and the web administrators of popular Uighur language websites, including the website *Misranim*, in the weeks leading up to Ramadan, Radio Free Asia reported in June. Ababekri Muhtar, the founder of *Misranim* and a disabled social activist, was also detained between April and June.

Authorities employed show trials, mass arrests, and sentencing to convict large numbers of Uighurs for state security and other suspected crimes. Seventeen Uighurs, including four women, were reportedly arrested in connection with a September incident that resulted in the death of a public security chief in Hotan prefecture, but there was no information on their alleged crimes or place of custody, according to NGOs.

Eleven Uighurs convicted of endangering state security and terrorism saw their sentences reduced or commuted by the Xinjiang High People's Court in February following lobbying efforts by the Dui Hua Foundation.

The government pressured foreign countries to repatriate or deny visas to Uighurs who had left the country, and repatriated Uighurs faced the risk of imprisonment and mistreatment upon return. There were accusations that government pressure led to India's cancellation of exiled Uighur leader Dolkun Isa's visa to attend a conference there, according to Reuters. Some Uighurs who were forcibly repatriated disappeared after arrival. The international community was still unable independently to confirm the welfare of the 109 Uighurs forcibly repatriated from Thailand in July 2015. Uighurs residing in Canada indicated that Xinjiang authorities detained and interrogated them during visits to the region, pressuring them to spy on other Uighurs living abroad for Chinese authorities.

Freedom of assembly was severely limited during the year in the XUAR. For information about abuse of religious freedom in Xinjiang, see the Department of State's *International Religious Freedom Report* at www.state.gov/religiousfreedomreport/.

Authorities did not permit possession of publications or audiovisual materials discussing independence, autonomy, or other politically sensitive subjects. Uighur Abduhelil Zunun remained in prison for his peaceful expression of ideas the government found objectionable.

The law criminalizes discussion of "separatism" on the internet and prohibits use of the internet in any way that undermines national unity. It further bans inciting ethnic separatism or "harming social stability" and requires internet service providers and network operators to set up monitoring systems or to strengthen existing ones and report violations of the law. Authorities reportedly searched cell phones at checkpoints and during random inspections of Uighur households, and those in possession of alleged terrorist material, including digital pictures of the East Turkistan flag, could be arrested and charged with crimes. When their use was detected, authorities forced individuals to delete messaging software and software used to circumvent internet filters. In some areas authorities restricted the use of cell phones and internet access. In February authorities in Chaghraq Township in Aksu Prefecture sentenced a resident to seven years in prison for allegedly watching a film on Muslim migration, according to a Radio Free Asia report.

For specific information on Tibet, see the Tibet Annex.

Acts of Violence, Discrimination, and Other Abuses Based on Sexual Orientation and Gender Identity

No laws criminalize private consensual same-sex activities between adults. Due to societal discrimination and pressure to conform to family expectations, most lesbian, gay, bisexual, transgender, and intersex (LGBTI) persons refrained from publicly discussing their sexual orientation or gender identity. Individuals and organizations working on LGBTI issues continued to report discrimination and harassment from authorities similar to that experienced by other organizations that accept funding from overseas.

Despite reports of domestic violence among LGBTI couples, the regulations on domestic violence and the Family Violence Law do not include same-sex partnerships, giving LGBTI victims of domestic violence less legal recourse than heterosexual victims.

Although homosexual activity is no longer officially pathologized, some mental health practitioners offered "corrective treatment" to LGBTI persons at "conversion therapy" centers or hospital psychiatric wards, sometimes at the behest of family members.

NGOs reported that although public advocacy work became more difficult for them in light of the Foreign NGO Management Law, they made some progress in advocating for LGBTI rights through specific antidiscrimination cases.

HIV and AIDS Social Stigma

Public health authorities reported there were more than 600,000 persons diagnosed with HIV in the country. New HIV diagnoses reported in 2015 numbered 115,465, up 11.5 percent from the 2014 total. During the year the government put significant efforts toward raising awareness of the risks of HIV/AIDS transmission, particularly among the college-age population, and Peng Liyuan made this problem a cornerstone of her platform as the country's "first lady."

Discrimination against persons with HIV remained a problem, impacting individuals' employment, educational, and housing opportunities and impeding access to health care. The law allows employers and schools to bar persons with infectious diseases and did not afford specific protections based on HIV status. During the year state media outlets reported instances of persons with HIV/AIDS who were barred from housing, education, or employment due to their HIV status.

A 2013 study by the Joint UN Program on HIV/AIDS conducted across seven provinces found that 53 percent of HIV-infected respondents who had recently been to a doctor were denied immediate treatment, often either being referred to an infectious disease hospital less equipped to handle ordinary medical problems or given alternate treatments. Some respondents said they chose to forgo medical treatment altogether rather than navigate obstacles imposed by the health-care system.

Inadequate protection for health-care workers exposed to HIV in the workplace was cited as a reason persons with HIV/AIDS faced challenges in the health-care system. In 2015 the National Health and Family Planning Commission sought to address the problem by issuing a regulation recognizing HIV exposure as an occupational hazard in certain professions, including medicine and public security. State media characterized the regulation in part as an effort to protect the rights of health workers better while curbing AIDS-related discrimination.

Other Societal Violence or Discrimination

The law prohibits discrimination against persons carrying infectious diseases and allows such persons to work as civil servants. The law does not address some common types of discrimination in employment, including discrimination based on height, physical appearance, or ethnic identity.

Despite provisions in the law, discrimination against hepatitis B carriers (including 20 million chronic carriers) remained widespread in many areas, and local governments sometimes tried to suppress their activities.

Despite a 2010 nationwide rule banning mandatory hepatitis B virus tests in job and school admissions applications, many companies continued to use hepatitis B testing as part of their pre-employment screening.

Section 7. Workers Right

a. Freedom of Association and the Right to Collective Bargaining

The law does not provide for freedom of association, and workers are not free to organize or join unions of their own choosing. Independent unions are illegal, and the right to strike is not protected in law. The law allows for collective wage bargaining for workers in all types of enterprises. The law further provides for industrial sector-wide or regional collective contracts, and enterprise-level collective contracts were generally compulsory throughout the country. Regulations require the government-controlled union to gather input from workers prior to consultation with management and to submit collective contracts to workers or their congress for approval. There is no legal obligation for employers to negotiate or to bargain in good faith, and some employers refused to do so.

The law provides legal protections against antiunion discrimination and specifies that union representatives may not be transferred or terminated by enterprise management during their term of office. The law provides for the reinstatement of workers dismissed for union activity as well as for other enterprise penalties for antiunion activities. The law does not protect workers who request or take part in collective negotiations with their employers independent of the officially recognized union. In several cases reported during the year, these workers faced reprisals including forced resignation, firing, and detention.

Only one union is recognized in law, the All China Federation of Trade Unions (ACFTU). All union activity must be approved by and organized under ACFTU, a CCP organ chaired by a member of the Politburo. The ACFTU and its provincial and local branches continued aggressively to establish new constituent unions and add new members, especially among migrant workers, in large, multinational enterprises. The law gives the ACFTU financial and administrative control over constituent unions empowered to represent employees in negotiating and signing collective contracts with enterprises and public institutions. The law does not mandate the ACFTU to represent the interests of workers in disputes.

The law provides for labor dispute resolution through a three-stage process: mediation between the parties, arbitration by officially designated arbitrators, and litigation. A key article of the law requires employers to consult with labor unions or employee representatives on matters that have a direct bearing on the immediate interests of their workers.

The law does not expressly prohibit work stoppages, and it is not illegal for workers to strike spontaneously. Authorities appeared most tolerant of strikes protesting unpaid or underpaid wages. Authorities rarely released statistics for labor disputes, but in November 2015 the official Xinhua News Agency reported a growing number of wage arrears cases totaling 11,007 in the first three quarters of 2015, an increase of 34 percent over the same period in 2014. Unofficial records from the Hong Kong-based labor rights NGO China Labor Bulletin (CLB) showed that at least 1,050 strikes and collective protests by workers occurred between December 2014 and February 2015, 90 percent relating to unpaid wages.

In some cases local authorities cracked down on such strikes, sometimes charging leaders with vague criminal offenses, such as "picking quarrels and provoking trouble," "disturbing public order," "damaging production operations," or detaining them without any charges at all. The only legally specified role for the ACFTU in strikes is to participate in investigations and assist the Ministry of Human Resources and Social Security in resolving disputes. There were, however, reports of cases in which ACFTU officials joined police in suppressing strikes.

Despite the appearances of a strong labor movement and relatively high levels of union registration, genuine freedom of association and worker representation did not exist. ACFTU constituent unions were generally ineffective in representing and protecting the rights and interests of workers. Workers generally did not see the ACFTU as an advocate, especially migrant workers who had the least interaction with union officials.

There were no publicly available official statistics on inspection efforts to enforce labor laws, and enforcement was generally insufficient to deter wide-scale violations. Labor inspectors lacked authority and resources to compel employers to correct violations. While the law outlines general procedures for resolving disputes, including mediation, arbitration, and recourse to the courts, procedures were lengthy and subject to delays. Local authorities in some areas actively sought to limit efforts by independent civil society and legal practitioners to offer organized advocacy, and some areas maintained informal quotas on the number of cases allowed to proceed beyond mediation.

The ACFTU and the CCP used a variety of mechanisms to influence the selection of trade union representatives. Although the law states that trade union officers at each level should be elected, most factory-level officers were appointed by ACFTU-affiliated unions, often in coordination with employers. Official union leaders often were drawn from the ranks of management. Direct election by workers of union leaders continued to be rare, occurred only at the enterprise level, and was subject to supervision by higher levels of the union or the CCP. In enterprises where direct election of union officers took place, regional ACFTU officers and local CCP authorities retained control over the selection and approval of candidates. Even in these cases, workers and NGOs expressed concern about the credibility of elections.

Employers often circumvented legal provisions allowing for collective consultation over wages, hours, days off, and benefits through such tactics as forcing employees to sign blank contracts and failing to provide workers with copies of their contracts.

There continued to be reports of workers throughout the country engaging in wildcat strikes, work stoppages, and other protest actions. Although the government restricted the release of statistics on the number of strikes and protests each year, the frequency of "spontaneous" strikes remained high, especially in Guangdong and other areas with developed labor markets and large pools of sophisticated, rights-conscious workers.

Coordinated efforts by governments at the central, provincial, and local levels, including harassment, detention, and the imposition of travel restrictions on labor rights defenders and restrictions on funding sources for NGOs, disrupted labor rights advocacy. In December 2015 police in Guangdong arrested Zeng Feiyang, director of the Panyu Workers' Center, for "gathering a crowd to disturb social order." Police also detained on similar charges six other workers' rights defenders: Zhu Xiaomei, Meng Han, and Tang Beiguo of the Panyu Dagongzu Service Center; Deng Xiaoming, a volunteer with the Haige Service Center; He Xiaobo of the Foshan Nanfeiyang Social Work Service Center; and Peng Jiayong of the Labor Mutual-aid Center. On September 26, a Guangdong court convicted Zeng Feiyang, Zhu Xiaomei, and Tang Beiguo of gathering a crowd to disturb social order and accepting funds from "foreign forces." They were given suspended prison sentences of between one and one-half and three years. On November 3, Meng Han was convicted and given a 21-month prison sentence. A local labor NGO said the court was sending a clear signal that the only way to resolve labor disputes was through government entities.

b. Prohibition of Forced or Compulsory Labor

The law prohibits forced and compulsory labor, and where there were reports that forced labor of adults and children occurred, the government reportedly enforced the law. Although the domestic media rarely reported forced labor cases and the penalties imposed, the law provides a penalty of imprisonment of not more than three years or criminal detention and a fine or, if the circumstances are serious, imprisonment of not less than three years but not more than 10 years and a fine. Men, women, and children were subjected to forced labor in coalmines and factories. In September, six men with mental disabilities were reportedly freed from a brick factory in Yunnan Province where they had been forced to work without pay. The brick kiln was shut down.

In 2013 the NPC abolished the Re-education Through Labor system, an arbitrary system of administrative detention without judicial review. Some media outlets and NGOs reported that forced labor continued in some drug rehabilitation facilities where individuals continued to be detained without judicial process. It was not possible independently to verify these reports.

Also see the Department of State's *Trafficking in Persons Report* at www.state.gov/j/tip/rls/tiprpt/.

c. Prohibition of Child Labor and Minimum Age for Employment

The law prohibits the employment of children under the age of 16. It refers to workers between the ages of 16 and 18 as "juvenile workers" and prohibits them from engaging in certain forms of dangerous work, including in mines.

The law specifies administrative review, fines, and revocation of business licenses of enterprises that illegally hire minors and provides that underage children found working be returned to their parents or other custodians in their original place of residence. The penalty for employing children under age 16 in hazardous labor or for excessively long hours ranges from three to seven years' imprisonment, but a significant gap remained between legislation and implementation. For example, in April media outlets reported that Wang Ningpan, a 15-year-old migrant worker from Hunan, died after working on the production line in an underwear garment factory in Foshan, Guangdong. Wang's normal work schedule was from 6 a.m. to 11 p.m. The garment factory gave Wang's family 155,000 yuan ($22,470) compensation. Official reports stated that Wang's mother had told the employer that her son was 17. Guangdong's provincial government launched an inspection to crack down on child labor, and the company was fined 10,000 yuan ($1,450) for hiring child labor.

Abuse of the student-worker system continued as well; as in past years, there were allegations that schools and local officials improperly facilitated the supply of student laborers.

d. Discrimination with Respect to Employment and Occupation

The Employment Promotion Law provides some basis for legal protection against employment discrimination. Article 3 states "no worker seeking employment shall suffer discrimination on the grounds of ethnicity, race, gender, or religious belief." Article 30 outlines employment protections available to carriers of infectious diseases. Enforcement clauses include the right to pursue civil damages through the courts. Other laws provide similar protections for women and persons with disabilities. The Labor Contract Law includes a provision limiting the circumstances under which employers could terminate the contracts of employees suspected of suffering from an occupational disease and those within five years of the statutory retirement age. The Ministry of Human Resources and Social Security and the local labor bureaus were responsible for verifying that enterprises complied with the labor laws and the employment promotion law.

Discrimination in employment was widespread, including in recruitment advertisements that discriminated based on gender, age, height, and physical appearance and health status (see section 6).

Some employers lowered the effective retirement age for female workers to 50. This reduced overall pension benefits, which were generally based on the number of years worked. Many employers preferred to hire men to avoid the expense of maternity leave.

Courts were generally reluctant to accept discrimination cases, and authorities at all levels emphasized negotiated settlements to labor disputes. As a result there were few examples of enforcement actions that resulted in final legal decisions. One example came from the Dongguan Municipal Intermediate People's Court's decision in May, which declared illegal a local department store's decision to revoke a female employee's paid maternity leave for a second child. The court ordered the company to restore the employee's position and to compensate her with 108 days of paid leave.

According to a study released in March, 50 percent of more than 10,000 female survey respondents working in 60 cities said they often experienced discrimination at the workplace, while 47 percent had encountered occasional discrimination and only 3 percent had never faced discrimination against them.

In 2015 authorities issued the Provisional Regulations for Residency. Effective from January, the provisional regulations require local authorities to establish a streamlined process for migrants to register as urban residents, renewable annually, and to provide and pay for a package of limited social service benefits for these new residents. The most important of the benefits would be the inclusion of compulsory education for the children of legal residents, meaning that children of migrant workers would be eligible to relocate with their parents and attend local urban schools. While the regulations would benefit many of the estimated 270 million migrant workers residing in urban centers, the unaltered half-century-old hukou system remained the most pervasive form of employment-related discrimination, denying migrant workers access to the full range of social benefits, including health care, pensions, and disability programs, on an equal basis with local residents.

e. Acceptable Conditions of Work

There was no national minimum wage, but the law generally requires local and provincial governments to set their own minimum wage rates for both the formal and informal sectors according to standards promulgated by the Ministry of Human Resources and Social Security. The law mandates a 40-hour standard workweek, excluding overtime, and a 24-hour weekly rest period. It also prohibits overtime work in excess of three hours per day or 36 hours per month and mandates premium pay for overtime work.

The State Administration for Work Safety sets and enforces occupational health and safety regulations. The law requires employers to provide free health checkups for employees working in hazardous conditions and to inform them of the results. The law also provides workers the right to report violations or remove themselves from workplace situations that could endanger their health without jeopardy to their employment.

Regulations state that labor and social security bureaus at or above the county level are responsible for enforcement of labor laws. The law also provides that, where the ACFTU finds an employer in violation of the regulation, it has the power to demand that the relevant local labor bureaus deal with the case. Companies that violate occupational, safety, and health regulations face various penalties, including suspension of business operations or rescission of business certificates and licenses.

The government did not effectively enforce the law. Penalties were not adequate to deter violations and were seldom enforced. The 230,000 inspectors were insufficient to monitor working conditions and did not operate in the informal sector. Despite many labor laws and regulations on worker safety, there were a number of workplace accidents during the year. Media and NGO reports attributed them to a lack of safety checks, weak enforcement of laws and regulations, ineffective supervision, and inadequate emergency responses.

Nonpayment of wages remained a problem in many areas. Governments at various levels continued efforts to prevent arrears and to recover payment of unpaid wages and insurance contributions. It remained possible for companies to relocate or close on short notice, often leaving employees without adequate recourse for due compensation.

Unpaid wages have been an acute problem in the construction sector for decades. Construction projects were often subcontracted several times until eventually a construction team composed of low-wage migrant workers was formed. This informal hiring scheme made rural laborers susceptible to delayed or unpaid payment for their work, prompting them to join in collective action. Workers occasionally took drastic measures to demand payment. In January the State Council issued guidance asking all government sectors to strengthen their efforts to solve the problem of migrant workers' unpaid wages and ordering the elimination of wage arrearage problems by 2020.

Workers in the informal sector often lacked coverage under labor contracts, and even with contracts, migrant workers in particular had less access to benefits, especially social insurance. Workers in the informal sector worked longer hours and earned one-half to two-thirds as much as comparable workers in the formal sector.

According to government sources, only an estimated 10 percent of eligible employees received regular occupational health services. Small and medium-sized enterprises, the country's largest group of employers, often failed to provide the required health services. They also did not provide proper safety equipment to help prevent disease and were rarely required to pay compensation to victims and their families.

Instances of pneumoconiosis, or black lung disease, and silicosis remained high. Official figures released in December 2015 showed the country recorded 26,873 new pneumoconiosis cases in 2014, a 16 percent increase from the previous year. The mining and processing of coal and nonferrous metals were the sectors most vulnerable to occupational diseases, responsible for 62.5 percent of all cases in 2015. In January the National Health and Family Planning Commission and 10 other ministry-level government organizations jointly issued a statement expressing concern over this workplace hazard. The statement noted that individuals were diagnosed with the disease at an increasingly younger age in recent years and that industries in central and western regions had become prone to the illness, mainly in jobs related to mining and handling construction materials and nonferrous metals.

On August 11, an explosion at a power plant in Dangyang, Hubei Province, killed 21 workers and severely injured five others. The blast, caused by the rupture of a steam pipe undergoing testing, came just a few hours before the first anniversary of the massive 2015 Tianjin warehouse explosion that killed 173 persons, including 104 firefighters. The CLB logged 37 explosions that were reported in the local media during the year, although major explosions, such as the one in Dangyang, were a small proportion of the overall number of workplace accidents.

Accidents tended to occur at the year-end, when employers and employees tended to overlook safety procedures to meet production goals. In the last quarter of the year, in addition to a November 24 scaffolding collapse in Jiangxi Province that killed 74 workers, media outlets reported a number of coal mine accidents, including an October 31 explosion at Chongqing that killed 33 workers, a December 1 accident at Qitaihe, Heilongjiang Province, that killed 21 miners, and a December 3 disaster in Inner Mongolia that left 32 persons dead.

Despite negative publicity surrounding the year-end increase, the number of workplace accidents and fatalities in the country decreased on a year-over-year basis. According to State Administration of Work Safety data, from 2010 to 2015, the number of accidents dropped from 363,383 to 281,576 and fatalities declined from 79,552 to 66,182. From January to October, 45,000 accidents occurred and 27,000 workers were killed, representing declines of 6.2 percent and 3.3 percent, respectively, from the same period in 2015. In addition, 23 major workplace accidents took place in the first eight months of the year, leaving 348 individuals dead or missing. The data represented year-over-year decreases of 11.5 percent and 32.8 percent, respectively.

TIBET 2016 HUMAN RIGHTS REPORT

EXECUTIVE SUMMARY

The United States recognizes the Tibet Autonomous Region (TAR) and Tibetan autonomous prefectures (TAPs) and counties in Sichuan, Qinghai, Yunnan, and Gansu Provinces to be a part of the People's Republic of China (PRC). The Chinese Communist Party's (CCP) Central Committee oversees Tibet policies. As in other predominantly minority areas of the PRC, ethnic Chinese CCP members held the overwhelming majority of top party, government, police, and military positions in the TAR and other Tibetan areas. Ultimate authority rests with the 25-member Political Bureau (Politburo) of the CCP Central Committee and its seven-member Standing Committee in Beijing, neither of which has any Tibetan members.

Civilian authorities generally maintained effective control over the security forces.

The government's respect for, and protection of, human rights in the TAR and other Tibetan areas remained poor. Under the professed objectives of controlling border areas, maintaining social stability, combating separatism, and extracting natural resources, the government engaged in the severe repression of Tibet's unique religious, cultural, and linguistic heritage by, among other means, strictly curtailing the civil rights of the Tibetan population, including the freedoms of speech, religion, association, assembly, and movement. The government routinely vilified the Dalai Lama and blamed the "Dalai [Lama] clique" and "other outside forces" for instigating instability.

Other serious human rights abuses included extrajudicial detentions, disappearances, and torture. Many Tibetans and other observers believed that authorities systemically targeted Tibetans for political repression, economic marginalization, and cultural assimilation, as well as educational and employment discrimination. The presence of the paramilitary People's Armed Police (PAP) and other security forces remained at high levels in many communities on the Tibetan Plateau, particularly in the TAR. Repression was severe throughout the year but increased in the periods before and during politically and religiously sensitive anniversaries and events. Authorities detained individuals in Tibetan areas after they reportedly protested against government or business actions or expressed their support for the Dalai Lama.

The government strictly controlled information about, and access to, the TAR and some key Tibetan areas outside the TAR, making it difficult to determine fully the scope of human rights problems. The Chinese government severely restricted free travel by foreign journalists to Tibetan areas. In addition, the Chinese government harassed or detained Tibetans who spoke to foreign reporters, attempted to provide information to persons abroad, or communicated information regarding protests or other expressions of discontent through cell phones, e-mail, or the internet. The few visits to the TAR by diplomats and journalists that were allowed were tightly controlled by local authorities. Because of these restrictions, many of the incidents and cases mentioned in this report could not be verified independently.

Disciplinary procedures were opaque, and there was no publicly available information to indicate that security personnel or other authorities were punished for behavior defined under PRC laws and regulations as abuses of power and authority.

Arbitrary Deprivation of Life and other Unlawful or Politically Motivated Killings

There were reports that the government or its agents committed arbitrary or unlawful killings. There were no reports that officials investigated or punished those responsible for such killings.

In June *Phayul.com* reported that Yudruk Nyima, a villager from Derge (Chinese: Dege) County, Kardze TAP in the Tibetan Region of Kham (Sichuan Province), was detained for reportedly "possessing a gun" and died in custody from injuries sustained through torture. According to local contacts, security forces in the local area raided many villages and monasteries and detained people to prevent them from celebrating the birthday of the Dalai Lama in early July.

Tibetan exiles and other observers believed Chinese authorities released Tibetan political prisoners in poor health to avoid deaths in custody. Lobsang Yeshi, a former village leader, died in a Lhasa hospital after enduring torture, mistreatment, and negligence at the hands of prison authorities, according to a July report by the Tibetan Center for Human Rights and Democracy. Authorities detained Lobsang Yeshi in 2014 after he protested against mining operations near his hometown.

In March Chinese authorities abruptly released Jigme Gyatso, a monk of Labrang Monastery who was serving a five-year criminal sentence on separatism charges, and moved him to a hospital in Lanzhou. According to Radio Free Tibet eyewitness reports, the monk was extremely frail due to repeated instances of severe torture, beatings, and poor conditions in the detention facilities.

Disappearance

Authorities in Tibetan areas continued to detain Tibetans arbitrarily for indefinite periods.

On June 30, according to the Tibetan Center for Human Rights and Democracy, Yeshi Lhakdron, a nun from Dragkar Nunnery in Kardze (Chinese: Ganzi) TAP in the Tibetan Region of Kham (Sichuan Province), who had been missing since her detention in 2008, reportedly died in police custody due to the effects of torture. Yeshi staged a peaceful protest in 2008 raising slogans such as "long live the Dalai Lama" and "freedom in Tibet."

The whereabouts of the 11th Panchen Lama, Gedhun Choekyi Nyima, Tibetan Buddhism's second-most prominent figure after the Dalai Lama, remained unknown. Neither he nor his parents have been seen since they were taken away by Chinese authorities in 1995 when he was only six years old.

Torture and Other Cruel and Degrading Treatment

Police and prison authorities employed torture and degrading treatment in dealing with some detainees and prisoners. There were many reports during the year that Chinese officials severely beat, even to the point of death, some Tibetans who were incarcerated or otherwise in custody.

On April 1, Radio Free Asia (RFA) reported that Tashi, a man from Chamdo TAP in the Tibetan Region of Kham, now administered by the TAR, was detained for unknown reasons just days before the March 10 anniversary of the 1959 Tibetan uprising. Sources reported that Tashi was driven to suicide due to being severely beaten and tortured while in detention.

On April 4, *Phayul.com* reported that Yeshi Dolma, a Tibetan political prisoner serving a 15-year sentence at the TAR's Drapchi Prison, was transferred to a hospital in Lhasa for urgent treatment. Yeshi was unable to stand without assistance, and sources say her disability was caused by torture and a lack of proper health care in prison. Authorities prohibited Yeshi's family and friends from meeting her at the hospital.

On May 13, *Phayul.com* reported that Lobsang Choedhar, a monk from Kirti Monastery in the Tibetan Region of Amdo located in Sichuan's Ngaba TAP, was in critical condition after enduring torture in prison. He was serving a 13-year sentence for calling for the return of the Dalai Lama and release of the Panchen Lama, Gendun Choekyi Nyima. According to local contacts, calls for the Chinese authorities to release him for medical treatment have been ignored.

In December Jigme Guri, a Tibetan political prisoner who had recently been released from prison, was admitted to a local government hospital in Sangchu County (Xiahe) in the Amdo Region of Tibet (Gansu Province). He had reportedly been subjected on four separate occasions to torture while in prison.

Prison and Detention Center Conditions

The number of prisoners in the TAR and Tibetan areas was unknown. There were reports of recently released prisoners permanently disabled or in extremely poor health because of the harsh treatment they endured in prison. Former prisoners reported being isolated in small cells for months at a time and deprived of sleep, sunlight, and adequate food. According to individuals who completed their prison terms during the year, prisoners rarely received medical care except in cases of serious illness. In April the TAR government stated that prisons in the region were tasked with re-educating prisoners who have endangered "state security" to strengthen the fight against separatism. There were many cases of detained and imprisoned persons being denied visitors. As elsewhere in the PRC, authorities did not permit independent monitoring of prisons.

Arbitrary Arrest or Detention

Arbitrary arrest and detention was a problem in Tibetan areas. Public security agencies are required by law to notify the relatives or employer of a detained person within 24 hours of the detention, but they often failed to do so when Tibetans and others were detained for political reasons. With a detention warrant, public security officers may legally detain persons throughout the PRC for up to 37 days without formally arresting or charging them. Following the 37-day period, public security officers must either formally arrest or release the detainee. Security officials frequently violated these requirements. It was unclear how many Tibetan detainees were held under forms of detention not subject to judicial review.

In May authorities in Kardze TAP in the Tibetan Region of Kham (Sichuan Province), detained 23-year-old Jampa Gelek after removing him from his monastery. According to RFA, authorities gave no reason for his detention, and he remained incarcerated at year's end.

In June authorities in Qinghai Province detained for a second time Choesang Gyatso, a monk from Lutsang monastery in the Tibetan Region of Amdo, just one day after authorities had freed him from a month of unexplained detention. Authorities provided no reason for the second detention, and he appeared to remain in detention at the end of the year. He started a civil organization to promote education among young Tibetan nomads and also edited a Tibetan cultural journal.

Denial of Fair Public Trial

Legal safeguards for detained or imprisoned Tibetans were inadequate in both design and implementation. Prisoners in China have the right to request a meeting with a government-appointed attorney, but many Tibetan defendants, particularly political defendants, did not have access to legal representation. In cases that authorities claimed involved "endangering state security" or "separatism," trials often were cursory and closed. Local sources noted that trials were predominantly conducted in Mandarin with government interpreters providing language services for Tibetan defendants who did not speak Mandarin. Court decisions, proclamations, and other judicial documents, however, were generally not published in Tibetan script.

Trial Procedures

In its annual work report, the TAR High People's Court stated it firmly fought against separatism and cracked down on the followers of "the 14th Dalai (Lama) clique," by, among other things, sentencing those who instigated protests, promoted separatism, and supported "foreign hostile forces."

According to a 2015 report in the government-controlled *Tibet Daily*, only 15 percent of the cadres (government and party officials) working for courts in the TAR had passed the National Legal Qualification Examination with a C grade certificate or higher. The report concluded that judges in the TAR were "strong politically, but weak professionally." In its 2016 annual work report, the TAR High People's Court stated that strengthening "political ideology" was the top priority of the court.

Security forces routinely subjected political prisoners and detainees known as "special criminal detainees" to "political re-education" sessions.

Political Prisoners and Detainees

An unknown number of Tibetans were detained, arrested, and sentenced because of their political or religious activity. Authorities held many prisoners in extrajudicial detention centers and never allowed them to appear in public court.

Based on information available from the political prisoner database of the Congressional-Executive Commission on China (CECC), as of August 1, 650 Tibetan political prisoners were known to be detained or imprisoned, most of them in Tibetan areas. Observers believed the actual number of Tibetan political prisoners and detainees to be much higher, but the lack of access to prisoners and prisons, as well as the dearth of reliable official statistics, made a precise determination difficult. An unknown number of persons continued to be held in detention centers rather than prisons. Of the 650 Tibetan political prisoners tracked by the CECC, 640 were detained in or after March 2008, and 10 were detained prior to March 2008. Of the 640 Tibetan political prisoners who were detained in or after March 2008, 276 were believed or presumed to be detained or imprisoned in Sichuan Province, 201 in the TAR, 95 in Qinghai Province, 67 in Gansu Province, and one in the Xinjiang Uighur Autonomous Region. There were 156 persons serving known sentences, which ranged from two years to life imprisonment. The average sentence length was eight years and seven months. Of the 156 persons serving known sentences, 69 were monks, nuns, or Tibetan Buddhist reincarnate teachers.

Tenzin Delek Rinpoche, an influential reincarnate lama and social activist, died in prison in 2015. Authorities immediately cremated the body without an autopsy or traditional religious funeral rites. According to local sources, the top priority for the followers of Tenzin Delek Rinpoche was to seek to identify his reincarnation, but officials prohibited his monasteries from conducting the search.

Tibetan Self-Immolations

Three Tibetans reportedly self-immolated during the year, including one Tibetan Buddhist monk and two laypersons, fewer than the seven self-immolations reported in 2015 and significantly fewer than the 83 self-immolations reported in 2012, bringing the total of self-immolations to at least 140 since 2009. Non-Chinese media reports stated that the declining number of reported self-immolations was due to tightened security by authorities and the collective punishment of self-immolators' relatives and associates, as well as the Dalai

Lama's public plea to his followers to find other ways to protest against Chinese government repression. Chinese officials in some Tibetan areas withheld public benefits from the family members of self-immolators and ordered friends and monastic personnel to refrain from participating in religious burial rites or mourning activities for self-immolators. According to a RFA report, security officials detained, beat, and tortured the wife and two daughters of Tashi Rabtan after he self-immolated in Gansu Province in December.

Self-immolators reportedly viewed their acts as protests against the government's political and religious oppression. The Chinese government implemented policies that punished friends, relatives, and associates of self-immolators. The Supreme People's Court, the Supreme People's Procuratorate, and the Ministry of Public Security's joint 2012 Opinion on Handling Cases of Self-immolation in Tibetan Areas According to Law criminalize various activities associated with self-immolation, including "organizing, plotting, inciting, compelling, luring, instigating, or helping others to commit self-immolation," each of which may be prosecuted as "intentional homicide." In September, 10 public security officers reportedly raided the home of Sangdak Kyab in Sangchu County (Xiahe) in the Amdo Region of Tibet (Gansu Province) and detained him in connection with the role he allegedly played in 2013, transporting the remains of a self-immolator to his family's home to prevent security agents from seizing the corpse.

On September 20, RFA reported that two monks of Labrang Monastery, Jinpa Gyatso and Kelsang Monlam, were sentenced to 18 months in prison in a secret trial by a court in Sangchu (Chinese: Xiahe) County in the Tibetan Region of Amdo (Gansu Province) for involvement in a 2015 self-immolation of another monk. The monks were arrested in June for sharing information and pictures of the self-immolation. Their families were not informed of the charges or of the monks' location after the arrests.

Arbitrary or Unlawful Interference with Privacy, Family, Home, or Correspondence

Since 2015 the TAR has strengthened the punishment of Communist Party members who follow the Dalai Lama, secretly harbor religious beliefs, make pilgrimages to India, or send their children to study with Tibetans in exile. Authorities continued to monitor private correspondence and search private homes and businesses for photographs of the Dalai Lama and other politically forbidden items. Police examined the cell phones of TAR residents to search for "reactionary music" from India and photographs of the Dalai Lama. Authorities also questioned and detained some individuals who disseminated writings and photographs over the internet.

On November 15, TAR CCP secretary Wu Yingjie outlined his plan to protect "social stability" that included a vow to "strictly implement a real-name user identification system for landline telephones, mobile phones, and the internet and continuously intensify the launching of attacks and specialized campaigns to counter and ferret out 'Tibetan independence' and promote the proliferation of party newspaper, journals, broadcasts, and television [programs] into every home in every village in order to completely stop infiltration by the hostile forces and the Dalai clique."

On February 24, *Phayul.com* reported that Gomar Choephel, a Tibetan monk from Rongwo Monastery in the Tibetan Region of Amdo (Qinghai Province), was sentenced to two years in prison in January for possessing a photograph of the Dalai Lama and sharing it on social media.

On December 6, a court in the Ngaba Tibetan and Qiang Autonomous Prefecture in the Tibetan Region of Amdo (Sichuan province) sentenced nine Tibetans to prison for terms ranging from five to 14 years for involvement in celebrations of the Dalai Lama's 80th birthday in 2015. Three of the nine, who were senior monks from Kirti Monastery, received the longest sentences of between 12 and 14 years each.

Freedom of Speech and Press

<u>Freedom of Speech and Expression</u>: Tibetans who spoke to foreign reporters, attempted to provide information to persons outside the country, or communicated information regarding protests or other expressions of discontent through cell phones, e-mail, or the internet were subject to harassment or detention under "crimes of undermining social stability and inciting separatism." During the year authorities in the TAR and other Tibetan areas sought to strengthen control over electronic media and to punish individuals for the ill-defined crime of "creating and spreading of rumors." According to official news reports in January, TAR officials punished 141 individuals for "creating and spreading rumors" online between June 2015 and January.

In March public security authorities charged Tashi Wangchuk, an entrepreneur and education advocate from Jyekundo in the Tibetan Region of Kham, now part of the Yushu TAP in Qinghai Province, with "inciting separatism," according to *The New*

York Times. Tashi's lawyer told the *Times* in August that public security case files he had reviewed indicated that the charge was based on Tashi's participation in a late 2015 *Times* report about the lack of Tibetan language education in Tibetan areas. Tashi was detained in January, but his family members were not informed until late March, and he remained in detention awaiting trial at the year's end. Tashi had no known record of advocating Tibetan independence or separatism, according to the *Times*, and has denied the charges against him.

On May 9, the Wenchuan County People's Court sentenced Jo Lobsang Jamyang, a monk at Kirti Monastery and a popular writer who addressed issues such as environmental protection and self-immolation protests, to seven years and six months in prison on charges of "leaking state secrets" and "engaging in separatist activities." The trial was closed, and his family and lawyers were barred from attending. Soon after he was detained in April 2015, 20 Tibetan writers jointly called for his release and praised his writings. Authorities held Jamyang incommunicado and reportedly tortured him during more than a year of pretrial detention.

On May 14, authorities detained Jamyang Lodroe, a monk from Tsinang Monastery in Ngaba TAP, without providing any information about his whereabouts or the reason for his detention to the monastery or to his family. Local sources told RFA reporters that it was widely believed that authorities detained Lodroe on account of his online publications.

Press and Media Freedoms: The government continued to severely restrict travel by foreign journalists. Foreign journalists may visit the TAR only after obtaining a special travel permit from the government, and this permission was rarely granted. The Foreign Correspondents Club of China's annual report stated that reporting from "Tibet proper remains off-limits to foreign journalists." This same report noted that many foreign journalists were also told that reporting in Tibetan areas outside the TAR was "restricted or prohibited."

Authorities tightly controlled journalists who worked for the domestic press and could hire and fire them on the basis of political reliability. In February TAR Television announced job vacancies with one of the listed job requirements to "be united with the regional party committee in political ideology and fighting against separatism." CCP propaganda authorities remained in charge of local journalist accreditation in the TAR and required journalists working in the TAR to display "loyalty to the Party and motherland." The deputy head of the TAR Propaganda Department simultaneously holds a prominent position in the TAR Journalist

Association, a state-controlled professional association to which local journalists must belong.

Violence and Harassment: Chinese authorities arrested and sentenced many Tibetan writers, intellectuals, and singers for "inciting separatism." In February the Malho (Hainan) Prefecture Intermediate People's Court in Qinghai Province sentenced Druklo (pen name: Shokjang), a writer and blogger from Labrang in the Tibetan Region of Amdo, to three years in prison for "inciting separatism." According to various sources, Shokjang wrote poetry and prose about Chinese government policies in Tibetan areas that enjoyed significant readership among Tibetans. Chinese security officials took Shokjang from the monastic center of Rebkong in March 2015, and no information was known about his welfare or whereabouts until the sentencing almost a year later.

Censorship or Content Restrictions: Domestic journalists were not allowed to report on repression in Tibetan areas. Authorities promptly censored the postings of bloggers who did so, and the authors sometimes faced punishment.

Since the establishment of the CCP's Central Leading Small Group for Internet Security and Informatization in 2014, the TAR Party Committee Information Office has further tightened the control of a full range of social media platforms. According to multiple contacts, security officials often cancelled WeChat accounts carrying "sensitive information," such as discussions about Tibetan language education, and interrogated the account owners. Many sources also reported that it was almost impossible to register websites promoting Tibetan culture and language in the TAR.

The Chinese government continued to jam radio broadcasts of Voice of America and RFA's Tibetan and Chinese-language services in some Tibetan areas as well as the Voice of Tibet, an independent radio station based in Norway. As part of a regular campaign cracking down on unauthorized radio and television channels, the TAR Department of Communications conducted an investigation in the Lhasa area in June and found zero "illegal radio programs."

According to multiple sources, authorities in Qinghai Province confiscated or destroyed "illegal" satellite dishes in many Tibetan areas. In addition to maintaining strict censorship of print and online content in Tibetan areas, Chinese authorities sought to censor the expression of views or distribution of information related to Tibet in countries outside the PRC. In February the PRC ambassador to Bangladesh pressured organizers of the Dhaka Art Summit to remove an exhibit that displayed the handwritten final writings of five Tibetans who had self-immolated in protest of Chinese government repression.

National Security: In 2015 China enacted a new National Security Law that includes provisions regarding the management of ethnic minorities and religion. The PRC frequently blamed "hostile foreign forces" for creating instability in Tibetan areas and cited the need to protect "national security" and "fight against separatism" as justifications for its policies, including censorship policies, in Tibetan areas.

Internet Freedom

Authorities curtailed cell phone and Internet service in the TAR and other Tibetan areas, sometimes for weeks or even months at a time, during periods of unrest and political sensitivity, such as the March anniversaries of the 1959 and 2008 protests, "Serf Emancipation Day," and around the Dalai Lama's birthday in July. When Internet service was restored, authorities closely monitored the Internet throughout Tibetan areas. Reports of authorities searching cell phones they suspected of containing suspicious content were widespread. Many individuals in the TAR and other Tibetan areas reported receiving official warnings after using their cell phones to exchange what the government deemed to be sensitive information.

In February the head of the TAR Party Committee Internet Information Office asserted that "the Internet is the key ideological battlefield between the TAR Party Committee and the 14th Dalai (Lama) clique."

In November the National People's Congress Standing Committee passed a cybersecurity law that further strengthened the legal mechanisms available to security agencies to surveil and control content online. Some observers noted that provisions of the law, such as Article 12, could disproportionally affect Tibetans and other ethnic minorities. Article 12 criminalizes using the internet to commit a wide range of ill-defined crimes of a political nature, such as "harming national security," "damaging national unity," "propagating extremism," "inciting ethnic hatred," "disturbing social order," and "harming the public interest." The law also codifies the practice of large-scale internet network shutdowns in response to "major [public] security incidents," which public security authorities in Tibetan areas have done for years without a clear basis in law. A work conference held in Lhasa on November 8 urged the TAR and other provinces with Tibetan areas to step up coordination in managing the internet.

Throughout the year, authorities blocked users in China from accessing foreign-based, Tibet-related websites critical of official government policy in Tibetan areas. Well-organized computer-hacking attacks originating from China harassed Tibet activists and organizations outside China.

Academic Freedom and Cultural Events

Authorities in many Tibetan areas required professors and students at institutions of higher education to attend regular political education sessions, particularly during politically sensitive months, in an effort to prevent "separatist" political and religious activities on campus. Authorities frequently encouraged Tibetan academics to participate in government propaganda efforts, such as making public speeches supporting government policies. Academics who refused to cooperate with such efforts faced diminished prospects for promotion.

Academics in the PRC who publicly criticized CCP policies on Tibetan affairs faced official reprisal. The government controlled curricula, texts, and other course materials as well as the publication of historically or politically sensitive academic books. Authorities frequently denied Tibetan academics permission to travel overseas for conferences and academic or cultural exchanges. Authorities in Tibetan areas regularly banned the sale and distribution of music they deemed to have sensitive political content.

In May senior officials of the state-run TAR Academy of Social Science encouraged scholars to maintain "a correct political and academic direction" and held a conference to "improve scholars' political ideology" and "fight against separatists."

Policies promoting planned urban economic growth, rapid infrastructure development, the influx of non-Tibetans to traditionally Tibetan areas, expansion of the tourism industry, forced resettlement of nomads and farmers, and the weakening of both Tibetan language education in public schools and religious education in monasteries continued to disrupt traditional living patterns and customs.

Tibetan and Mandarin Chinese are official languages in the TAR, and both languages appeared on some, but not all, public and commercial signs. Inside official buildings and businesses, including banks, post offices, and hospitals, signage in Tibetan was frequently lacking, and in many instances forms and documents were available only in Mandarin. Mandarin was used for most official communications and was the predominant language of instruction in public schools in many Tibetan areas. Private printing businesses in Chengdu needed special government approval to print in the Tibetan language.

A small number of public schools in the TAR continued to teach mathematics in the Tibetan language, but in June the *Tibet Post* reported that TAR officials have replaced Tibetan language mathematics textbooks in all regional schools with Mandarin versions. Sources reported that WeChat users in the TAR discussing the issue were subsequently visited by public security officers and given warnings.

According to sources, there were previously 20 Tibetan language schools or workshops for local children operated by Tibetan Buddhist monasteries in Sichuan Province's Kardze TAP. After the 2015 release of the Kardze TAP Relocation Regulation for Minors in Monasteries, authorities forced 15 of these schools to close and relocated their students to government-run schools.

The Kardze TAP has the highest illiteracy rate (above 30 percent) in Sichuan Province, compared with a national rate of 4 to 5 percent. Despite the illiteracy problem, in late April the central government ordered the destruction of much of Larung Gar, the largest Tibetan Buddhist education center, a focal point for promoting both Tibetan and Chinese literacy.

China's Regional Ethnic Autonomy Law states that "schools (classes and grades) and other institutions of education where most of the students come from minority nationalities shall, whenever possible, use textbooks in their own languages and use their languages as the media of instruction." Despite guarantees of cultural and linguistic rights, many primary, middle, high school, and college students had limited access to Tibetan language instruction and textbooks, particularly in the areas of modern education.

China's most prestigious universities provided no instruction in Tibetan or other ethnic minority languages, although classes teaching the Tibetan language were available at a small number of universities. "Nationalities" universities, established to serve ethnic minority students and ethnic Chinese students interested in ethnic minority subjects, offered Tibetan language instruction only in courses focused on the study of the Tibetan language or culture. Mandarin was used in courses for jobs that required technical skills and qualifications.

Freedom of Assembly and Association

Even in areas officially designated as "autonomous," Tibetans generally lacked the right to organize and play a meaningful role in the protection of their cultural heritage and unique natural environment. Tibetans often faced intimidation and arrest if they protested against policies or practices they found objectionable. A 2015 RFA report stated that authorities in Rebkong County in the Tibetan Region of Amdo, now administered under Qinghai Province, circulated a list of unlawful activities. The list included "illegal associations formed in the name of the Tibetan language, the environment, and education." Sources in the area reported that this list remained in force and no new associations have been formed since the list was published.

In February 2015 public security officials in Chengdu, the capital of Sichuan Province, detained a group of Tibetans who were peacefully protesting the government's seizure of land in Zoige County in the Tibetan Region of Amdo, now administered by Sichuan, outside a meeting of the Sichuan Provincial People's Congress. In April four of these Tibetans were sentenced to prison terms of two to three years.

On June 23, a protest by Tibetans on Qinghai Lake over the demolition of unregistered restaurants and guest houses was violently dispersed by security forces, leading to the arrest of five demonstrators and the injury of at least eight others. Authorities decreed that these small businesses were illegal and needed to be torn down and that residents should leave the area, which was a popular tourist location. Local Tibetans likened it to a "land grab" meant to benefit ethnic Chinese at their expense.

At the Sixth Tibet Work Forum in August 2015, the CCP ordered a large-scale campaign to expel students and demolish living quarters at Larung Gar, the world's largest center for the study of Tibetan Buddhism. The expulsion and demolition campaign commenced in July. According to a local CCP directive, authorities must reduce the resident population to no more than 5,000 by September 2017. Before the campaign began, the population at Larung Gar was estimated to range between 10,000 and 30,000. In July authorities banned foreign tourists from visiting the area.

In August authorities in the Kardze TAP in the Tibetan Region of Kham reportedly prevented Tibetans from holding a religious gathering and traditional horse race festival after Dargye Monastery, the organizer of the events, and local residents refused a government order to fly the PRC national flag at the two events, at the monastery, and from residents' homes.

Freedom of Religion

See the Department of State's *International Religious Freedom Report* at www.state.gov/religiousfreedomreport/.

Freedom of Movement

Chinese law provides for freedom of internal movement, foreign travel, emigration, and repatriation; however, the government severely restricted travel and freedom of movement for Tibetans, particularly Tibetan Buddhist monks and nuns.

<u>In-country Movement</u>: Freedom of movement for all Tibetans, but particularly for monks and nuns, remained severely restricted throughout the TAR, as well as in other Tibetan areas. The PAP and local public security bureaus set up roadblocks and checkpoints on major roads, in cities, and on the outskirts of cities and monasteries, particularly around sensitive dates. Tibetans traveling in monastic attire were subject to extra scrutiny by police at roadside checkpoints and at airports.

Authorities sometimes banned Tibetans, particularly monks and nuns, from going outside the TAR and from traveling to the TAR without first obtaining special permission from multiple government offices. Many Tibetans reported encountering difficulties in obtaining the required permissions. This not only made it difficult for Tibetans to make pilgrimages to sacred religious sites in the TAR, but also obstructed land-based travel to India through Nepal. Tibetans from outside the TAR who traveled to Lhasa also reported that authorities there required them to surrender their national identification cards and notify authorities of their plans in detail on a daily basis. These requirements were not applied to ethnic Chinese visitors to the TAR.

Even outside the TAR, many Tibetan monks and nuns reported that it remained difficult to travel beyond their home monasteries for religious and traditional Tibetan education, with officials frequently denying permission for visiting monks to stay at a monastery for religious education. Implementation of this restriction was especially rigorous in the TAR, and it undermined the traditional Tibetan Buddhist practice of seeking advanced teachings from a select number of senior teachers based at major monasteries scattered across the Tibetan Plateau.

<u>Foreign Travel</u>: Many Tibetans continued to report difficulties in obtaining new or renewing existing passports. Sources reported that Tibetans and other minorities had to provide far more extensive documentation than other Chinese citizens when applying for a Chinese passport. In the TAR, a scholar needs to get about seven stamps with signatures from various government offices to apply for a passport, in addition to other standard required documentation. For Tibetans, the passport application process could take years and frequently ended in rejection. Some Tibetans reported they were able to obtain passports only after paying substantial bribes. Tibetans continued to encounter substantial difficulties and obstacles in traveling to India for religious, educational, and other purposes. Individuals also reported instances of local authorities revoking their passports after they had returned to China.

In November Chinese officials in the Tibetan Regions of Kham and Amdo under the administration of Qinghai, Sichuan, and Gansu Provinces visited the homes of Tibetan passport holders and confiscated their documents, according to an RFA report. Officials claimed the passports were collected in order to affix new seals on them, but Tibetans suspected the timing was intended to make it impossible for them to attend an important religious ceremony known as the Kalachakra, which the Dalai Lama planned to conduct in India in January 2017. Additional reports in December indicated that travel agencies in China were told explicitly by local authorities to cancel trips to India and Nepal during this same period. The apparent travel ban also reportedly extended to ethnic Chinese travelers. Tibetans who had traveled to Nepal and planned to continue on to India reported that Chinese officials visited their homes in Tibet and threatened their relatives if they did not return immediately. Sources reported that explicit punishments included placing family members on a blacklist, which could lead to the loss of a government job or difficulty in finding employment; expulsion of children from the public education system; and revocation of national identification cards, thereby preventing access to other social services, such as health care and government aid.

Tight border controls sharply limited the number of persons crossing the border into Nepal and India. In 2015, 89 Tibetan refugees transited Nepal through the Tibetan Reception Center, run by the Office of the UN High Commissioner for Refugees in Kathmandu, en route to permanent settlement in India. This compared with 80 in 2014, down from 171 in 2013 and 242 in 2012.

The government restricted the movement of Tibetans in the period before and during sensitive anniversaries and events and increased controls over border areas at these times. In February there were reports that travel agents in Chengdu were forbidden to sell package overseas tours to Tibetans for the months of March and July, the periods of time around Tibet Uprising Day (March 10) and the Dalai Lama's birthday (July 6).

The government regulated travel by foreigners to the TAR, a restriction not applied to any other provincial-level entity in the PRC. In accordance with a 1989 regulation, foreign visitors had to first obtain an official confirmation letter issued by the TAR government before entering the TAR. Most tourists obtained such letters by booking tours through officially registered travel agencies. In the TAR, a government-designated tour guide had to accompany foreign tourists at all times. It was rare for foreigners to obtain permission to enter the TAR by road. In what has become an annual practice, authorities banned many foreign tourists from the TAR in the period before and during the March anniversary of the 1959 Tibetan uprising. Foreign tourists sometimes also faced restrictions traveling to Tibetan areas outside the TAR.

The decline in the number of foreign tourists to the TAR was more than offset by an increase in domestic ethnic Chinese visitors to the TAR. Unlike foreign tourists, Chinese tourists did not need special permits to visit the TAR.

Officials continued to tightly restrict the access of foreign diplomats and journalists to the TAR. Foreign officials were able to travel to the TAR only with the permission of the TAR Foreign Affairs Office, and even then only on closely chaperoned trips arranged by that office. With the exception of a few highly controlled trips, authorities repeatedly denied requests for international journalists to visit the TAR and other Tibetan areas (see section on Freedom of Speech and Press).

In September *The Washington Post* reported that "the Tibet Autonomous Region, as China calls central Tibet, is harder to visit as a journalist than North Korea. There were only a handful of government tours organized for journalists in the past decade, all closely controlled."

Freedom to Participate in the Political Process

According to the law, Tibetans and other Chinese citizens have the right to vote in some local elections. In practice the Chinese government severely restricted its citizens' ability to participate in any meaningful elections.

In 2015 RFA reported that security forces in Kyangchu Village in Qinghai Province detained nearly 70 Tibetans who had protested against local officials' insistence that villagers vote for the local government's preferred candidate in a village election. Sources reported that those detainees were subsequently released, but they were prohibited from voting in village elections.

Since 2015 the TAR and many Tibetan areas have reinforced implementation of the Regulation for Village Committee Management, which stipulates that the primary condition for participating in any local election is the "willingness to resolutely fight against separatism;" in some cases, this condition is interpreted to require candidates to denounce the Dalai Lama. Many villagers in Tibetan areas of Sichuan and Qinghai Provinces expressed frustration that the best candidates for village heads were unwilling to run under those conditions. According to many scholars, the regulation led to high turnover during the year: As a result, 90 percent of TAR township and village-level leaders as well as delegates to the local People's Congress, were new; the same was true for 70 percent of those in Qinghai Province.

Corruption and Lack of Transparency in Government

The law provides criminal penalties for corrupt acts by officials, but the government did not implement the law effectively in Tibetan areas, and officials often engaged in corrupt practices with impunity. There were numerous reports of government corruption in Tibetan areas during the year.

Discrimination, Societal Abuses, and Trafficking in Persons

Women

Rape and Domestic Violence: There was no confirmed information on the incidence of rape or domestic violence.

Reproductive Rights: Population and birth planning policies permitted Tibetans and members of some other minority groups to have more children than Han Chinese. Prostitution involving local women in Tibetan areas was not uncommon. Nongovernmental organizations and health experts expressed serious concern about the growing prevalence of HIV/AIDS in the TAR and other Tibetan areas.

Discrimination: There were no formal restrictions on women's participation in the political system, and women held many lower-level government positions. They were, however, underrepresented at the provincial and prefectural levels of government.

According to official reports, female government and party officials in the TAR have accounted for 41 percent of the TAR's total cadres since 2012. During the year the TAR was the only provincial-level jurisdiction in the PRC that did not have at least one female cadre in its provincial CCP standing committee.

Children

Many rural Tibetan areas have implemented China's nationwide "centralized education" policy, which has resulted in the closure of many village and monastic schools and the transfer of students, including elementary school students, to boarding schools in towns and cities. Reports indicated many of the boarding schools did not adequately care for and supervise their young students. This policy also resulted in diminished acquisition of the Tibetan language and culture by removing Tibetan children from their homes and communities where the Tibetan language is used.

Trafficking in Persons

See the Department of State's annual *Trafficking in Persons Report* at www.state.gov/j/tip/rls/tiprpt/.

Ethnic Minorities

Although the 2010 TAR census figures showed that Tibetans made up 90.5 percent of the TAR's permanently registered population, official figures did not include a large number of long-, medium-, and short-term ethnic Chinese migrants, such as cadres, skilled and unskilled laborers, military and paramilitary troops, and their respective dependents. Tibetans continued to make up nearly 98 percent of those registered as permanent residents in rural areas, according to official census figures.

Migrants to the TAR and other parts of the Tibetan Plateau were overwhelmingly concentrated in urban areas. Government policies to subsidize economic development often benefited ethnic Chinese migrants more than Tibetans. In many predominantly Tibetan cities across the Tibetan Plateau, ethnic Chinese or Hui migrants owned and managed most of the small businesses, restaurants, and retail shops.

According to a December CNN report, Tibetans in the TAR were paid less than Han Chinese migrants there. A Tibetan laborer was quoted indicating Tibetan laborers received on average two-thirds the pay of ethnic Chinese for the same work.

Observers continued to express concern that development projects and other central government policies disproportionately benefited non-Tibetans and resulted in a considerable influx of Han Chinese and Hui persons into the TAR and other Tibetan areas. Many major infrastructure projects across the Tibetan Plateau were engineered and implemented by large state-owned enterprises based in other provinces, and they were managed and staffed by professionals and low-wage temporary migrant workers from other provinces rather than by local residents.

Economic and social exclusion was a major source of discontent among a varied cross section of Tibetans. Some Tibetans continued to report discrimination in employment. Some Tibetans reported it was more difficult for Tibetans than ethnic Chinese to obtain permits and loans to open businesses. Restrictions on both local NGOs that received foreign funding and international NGOs that provided assistance to Tibetan communities increased during the year, resulting in a decrease of beneficial NGO programs in the TAR and other Tibetan areas.

The government continued its campaign to resettle Tibetan nomads into urban areas and newly created communities in rural areas across the TAR and other Tibetan areas. Despite a January 2014 Xinhua News Agency report that claimed the TAR's eight-year nomad resettlement program was officially completed at the end of 2013, there were new reports of compulsory resettlement. Improving housing conditions, health care, and education for Tibet's poorest persons were among the stated goals of resettlement, although there was a pattern of settling herders near townships and roads and away from monasteries, which were the traditional providers of community and social services. A requirement that herders bear a substantial part of the resettlement costs often forced resettled families into debt.

Although a 2015 media report noted that Tibetans and other minority ethnic groups made up 70 percent of government employees in the TAR, the top CCP position of TAR party secretary continued to be held by a Han Chinese, and the corresponding positions in the vast majority of all TAR counties were also held by Han Chinese. Within the TAR, Han Chinese also continued to hold a disproportionate number of the top security, military, financial, economic, legal, judicial, and educational positions. Han Chinese were party secretaries in eight of the nine TAPs, which are located in Gansu, Qinghai, Sichuan, and Yunnan Provinces. One TAP in Qinghai Province had a Tibetan party secretary. Authorities strictly prohibited Tibetans holding government and CCP positions from openly worshipping at monasteries or otherwise publicly practicing their religion.

Government propaganda against alleged Tibetan "proindependence forces" contributed to Chinese societal discrimination against ordinary Tibetans. Many Tibetan monks and nuns chose to wear nonreligious clothing to avoid harassment when traveling outside their monasteries and throughout China. Some Tibetans reported that taxi drivers throughout China refused to stop for them and hotels refused to give them rooms.

HONG KONG 2016 HUMAN RIGHTS REPORT

EXECUTIVE SUMMARY

Hong Kong is a special administrative region (SAR) of the People's Republic of China (PRC). The 1984 Sino-British Joint Declaration on the Question of Hong Kong and the SAR's charter, the Basic Law of the SAR (also known as the Basic Law), specify that the SAR will enjoy a high degree of autonomy under the "one country, two systems" framework except in matters of defense and foreign affairs. In September, Hong Kong residents elected the 70 representatives who comprise the SAR's Legislative Council (LegCo). In accordance with the Basic Law, voters directly elected 40 representatives, while limited franchise functional constituencies that generally supported the government in Beijing elected the remaining 30.

Civilian authorities maintained effective control over the security forces.

The most important human rights problem reported was the central government's encroachment on Hong Kong's autonomy. The National People's Congress Standing Committee (NPCSC) on November 7 issued an unnecessary and unsolicited interpretation of the Basic Law that preempted the ability of Hong Kong's independent judiciary to rule on the matter. It marked the first time it had issued such an interpretation while a Hong Kong judge was deliberating the case in question and the second time it had done so in the absence of a request from Hong Kong authorities. As a result, Hong Kong's courts subsequently disqualified two opposition legislators-elect, who used their oath-swearing ceremony as an occasion to make proindependence gestures, and on December 2, the Hong Kong government filed a similar legal challenge to the legitimacy of four additional opposition legislators over the manner in which they took their oaths of office. Media outlets and local observers raised concerns that the government had attempted to curtail residents' right to run for office. Hong Kong residents also remain concerned by the breach of Hong Kong's autonomy that occurred in the late 2015 disappearances of five publishers of books critical of the Communist Party leadership and the continued lack of transparency regarding their cases. Although the 2016 elections were largely conducted in a free and fair manner, Hong Kong's system of government limits the ability of Hong Kong voters to choose their government.

Other human rights problems included trafficking in persons, and societal prejudice against certain ethnic minorities and the lesbian, gay, bisexual, transgender, and intersex (LGBTI) community.

The government took steps to prosecute and punish officials who committed abuses.

Section 1. Respect for the Integrity of the Person, Including Freedom from:

a. Arbitrary Deprivation of Life and other Unlawful or Politically Motivated Killings

There were no reports that the government or its agents committed arbitrary or unlawful killings; nor were there reports of such killings by narcotics traffickers or other criminal groups.

b. Disappearance

Five men working in Hong Kong's publishing industry disappeared between October and December 2015 from Thailand, Hong Kong, and mainland China. In addition to being Hong Kong residents, one of the men was a Swedish national and another was a UK national. Media coverage of these cases noted the men worked for Mighty Current, a publishing house, and the affiliated Causeway Bay Bookstore, which were known for selling books critical of the Chinese Communist Party and its leaders. Credible reports gave rise to widespread suspicions that PRC security officials were involved in their disappearances.

Mainland authorities eventually allowed four of the five booksellers to return to Hong Kong between March and July, while continuing to detain Gui Minhai, a Swedish national, on the mainland at year's end in the absence of any charges or judicial process. According to local media reports, mainland security agencies continued to exert pressure on the four booksellers whom they had allowed to return to Hong Kong through periodic questioning, ongoing surveillance, escorting by security agents, and threats of retaliation against mainland-based family members. Causeway Bay Books manager Lam Wing-kee returned to Hong Kong in July and held a press conference at the LegCo compound in which he disclosed details about his abduction and subsequent eight-month detention. Lam said several security agents took him into custody at the Hong Kong-Shenzhen border crossing and held him overnight. According to Lam's account, mainland authorities confiscated his identity documents and refused to answer his questions or explain why he was detained. The next day officials blindfolded and handcuffed Lam on central authorities' orders, following which Lam was transported by train from Shenzhen to Ningbo. Upon arrival in Ningbo, security officials forced Lam to sign a document promising to not contact his family or seek legal counsel, he told the press. He was told he was being held under "residential surveillance," a form of detention frequently used by PRC security agents to hold incommunicado activists and others suspected of political crimes. Lam said he was held under constant surveillance in a small space, and told the press he was only released to return to the SAR in order to collect additional materials for use in testifying against another bookseller.

The Hong Kong Government said it took steps to investigate the booksellers' abductions and detentions, including engaging central government authorities from the security and justice ministries to improve the notification mechanism governing cross-border cases. The Chief Executive, Secretary for Justice, Police Commissioner, and Central Government Liaison Officials, in addition to other key officers, spoke publicly following UK national Lee Bo's disappearance. They all stated unequivocally that mainland security officials had no legal ability to enforce mainland laws in Hong Kong. Top officials, including the Chief Executive, said if mainland officials had acted in Hong Kong, it would be a violation of the Basic Law.

Despite the Hong Kong authorities' efforts to pursue the case, police eventually dropped their investigation following the Lee family's cancellation of its missing person report and the family's request for closure of the investigation.

c. Torture and Other Cruel, Inhuman, or Degrading Treatment or Punishment

The Basic Law prohibits torture and other forms of abuse, and there were no reports that government officials employed them.

There were some reports of the use of excessive force by police officers. In a six-month period last year, the police force's Complaints against Police Office reported 913 allegations of excessive use of force by police. Data on allegations of excessive use of force pending investigation and endorsement by the Independent Police Complaints Council (IPCC), assault by police officers on persons not in custody and in custody, and the results of those investigations were not available at year's end. There were no reports of death in custody due to excessive police force.

Prison and Detention Center Conditions

Prison and detention center conditions generally met international standards, and the Correctional Services Department (CSD) permitted visits by independent human rights observers, the media, and religious groups.

The government does not have separate detention facilities for migrants or asylum seekers. The Immigration Department maintains detention facilities in Ma Tau Kok and in Castle Peak Bay for those who have violated the SAR's immigration laws and/or those pending deportation from Hong Kong. Human rights activists voiced concern over the government's detention of asylum claimants at such immigration detention facilities, charging that the SAR's immigration laws require asylum claimants to be in violation of their immigration status before they can file an asylum claim. There are no private detention facilities in the SAR.

Physical Conditions: During the year the CSD managed 24 penal institutions (comprising minimum-, medium-, and maximum-security prisons; a psychiatric center; and training, detention, rehabilitation, and drug addiction treatment centers).

The CSD acknowledged overcrowding was a problem in certain types of penal institutions, such as remand (pretrial detention) facilities and maximum-security institutions. Transferred remand prisoners made complaints of prison guards treating them as convicted prisoners as well as of wait times of one week to make private telephone calls, and reported a decrease in attorney visits for prisoners relocated to some of the SAR's more remote prison locations. The CSD adopted a strategy of renovating existing institutions to increase space and modernize facilities.

The Coroner's Court, aided by a jury, conducted death inquests. Data on deaths of prisoners in CSD custody and inquest results had not been reported by year's end.

Administration: Judicial authorities investigated credible allegations of problematic conditions and documented the results in a publicly accessible manner. The government investigated and monitored prison and detention center conditions, and there was an external Office of the Ombudsman. The government kept adequate records of prisoners.

<u>Independent Monitoring</u>: The government permitted media outlets and human rights groups to conduct prison visits. Justices of the peace may make suggestions and comments on matters such as the physical environment of facilities, overcrowding, staff improvement, training and recreational programs and activities, and other matters affecting the welfare of inmates. Justices of the peace made over 200 unannounced visits to penal institutions in a six-month period last year.

<u>Improvements</u>: As of year's end, there was no available information on improvements to prison or detention center conditions.

d. Arbitrary Arrest or Detention

The law prohibits arbitrary arrest or detention, and the government generally observed these prohibitions.

Role of the Police and Security Apparatus

The Hong Kong Police Force maintains internal security and reports to the Security Bureau. The People's Liberation Army (PLA) is responsible for external security. The Immigration Department controls the entry of persons into and out of the SAR as well as the documentation of local residents. Civilian authorities maintained effective control over the police force, and the government had effective mechanisms to investigate and punish abuse and corruption. The 2015 reported involvement of mainland security forces in the disappearances of five Hong Kong book publishers; however, raised concerns about the activities of mainland security forces in Hong Kong throughout the year. For further information on the publishers' cases, see section 1.b.

International and local media reported that mainland PRC operatives in Hong Kong surveilled some prodemocracy movement figures, political activists, lawyers, academics, businesspersons, and religious leaders that have expressed criticism of the central government's policies. In January, Guangdong province security agents reportedly visited 65-year-old veteran publisher Lau Tat-man in Hong Kong on three occasions over the course of one month to interrogate him about the five booksellers who were abducted from various locations and detained in the mainland. In July bookseller Lam Wing-kee and prodemocracy legislator James To alleged that mainland agents had surveilled Lam after he returned to Hong Kong and disclosed the details of his abduction to the press. In response to concerns for his safety, Hong Kong police later placed Lam under police protection. There were no reports of impunity involving the security forces during the year.

Human rights activists and some legislators expressed concern that the CE appointed all Independent Police Complaints Committee members and that the IPCC's lack of power to conduct independent investigations limited its oversight capacity. The IPCC cannot compel officers to participate in its investigations, and the media reported cases of police officers declining to cooperate fully.

Arrest Procedures and Treatment of Detainees

Suspects generally were apprehended openly with warrants based on sufficient evidence and issued by a duly authorized official. They must be charged within 48 hours or released, and the government respected this right. Interviews of suspects are required to be videotaped. The law provides accused persons with the right to a prompt judicial determination, and authorities respected this right effectively.

Detainees were generally informed promptly of charges against them. There was a functioning bail system, and authorities allowed detainees access to a lawyer of their choice. Suspects were not detained incommunicado or held under house arrest.

Arbitrary Arrest: The Department of Justice maintained political considerations did not factor into its decision to charge several activists with crimes related to the 2014 protests; the Hong Kong judiciary heard these cases from May to August. Pro-democracy activists and participants in the fall 2014 prodemocracy protests claimed they were subject to incidents of politically motivated arbitrary arrest.

In May, Joshua Wong, the convener of the prodemocracy student activist group Scholarism, and Hong Kong Federation of Students (HKFS) secretary-general Nathan Law, along with two other prodemocracy activists, were acquitted on charges related to obstructing police officers during a June 2014 protest against the release of the State Council's White Paper on Hong Kong.

In July, Wong and HKFS former secretary-general Alex Chow were found guilty on one charge of participating in an illegal assembly related to the start of the 2014 Occupy Central protests, while Law was found guilty of inciting an illegal assembly. In August, Wong and Law were sentenced to perform 80 and 120 hours of community service respectively, while Chow was given a suspended sentence of three weeks imprisonment. In delivering the verdicts, district court Judge June

Cheung noted: "The court believes the three defendants are expressing their views and demands genuinely out of their political beliefs or their concern for society. Their aim and motive is not for their own interest or to hurt other people."

The Department of Justice in September requested the court review the sentences, with the prosecution alleging the sentences were too lenient. The magistrate reviewed and upheld the sentences, which fell well within sentencing guidelines.

Many experts assessed the police use of force during the protests in the fall of 2014 as generally professional and appropriate. Some prodemocracy activists, nongovernmental organization (NGO) observers, and journalists expressed concerns about certain police actions, and the court cases reviewing police use of force continued.

The District Court on December 8 announced it would hand down a ruling in February 2017 on an assault case brought by Ken Tsang, a prodemocracy activist. Video footage taken during October 2014 protests showed plainclothes police officers abusing Tsang. Seven police officers were subsequently suspended, arrested, and charged with the crime of "wounding or striking with intent to do grievous bodily harm." Prosecutors separately charged Tsang with assaulting and obstructing police officers, which carries a maximum possible sentence of two years' imprisonment. The court finished hearing the case in May, and Tsang was found guilty of assaulting a police officer and resisting arrest; he was sentenced to five weeks in prison.

Detainee's Ability to Challenge Lawfulness of Detention before a Court: Persons arrested or detained on criminal or other grounds are entitled to challenge in court the legal basis or arbitrary nature of their detention and obtain prompt release and compensation if found to have been unlawfully detained.

e. Denial of Fair Public Trial

The law provides for an independent judiciary, and the SAR government generally respected judicial independence. The judiciary provided citizens with a fair and efficient judicial process.

Trial Procedures

The law provides for the right to a fair public trial, and an independent judiciary generally enforced this right. Trials were by jury except at the magistrate and district court level. An attorney is provided at the public's expense if defendants cannot afford counsel. Defendants had adequate time and facilities to prepare a defense. Defendants have the right to be informed promptly and in detail of the charges against them and the right to a public trial without undue delay, and defendants could confront and question witnesses testifying against them and present witnesses to testify on their behalf. Defendants and their attorneys had access to government-held evidence relevant to their cases. Defendants have the right of appeal and the right not to be compelled to testify or confess guilt, and have the right to be present at their trial.

Defendants enjoy a presumption of innocence except in official corruption cases. Under the law a current or former government official who maintained a standard of living above that commensurate with his or her official income, or who controls monies or property disproportionate to his official income, is guilty of an offense unless he can satisfactorily explain the discrepancy. The courts upheld this ordinance. The government conducted court proceedings in either Chinese or English, the SAR's two official languages.

Hong Kong's unique, common law judicial system operates within the PRC; the SAR's courts are charged with interpreting those provisions of the Basic Law that address matters within the limits of the SAR's autonomy. The courts also interpret provisions of the Basic Law that touch on central government responsibilities or on the relationship between the central authorities and the SAR. Before making its final judgments on these matters, which are not subject to appeal, the Court of Final Appeal may seek an interpretation of the relevant provisions from the Standing Committee of the PRC's National People's Congress (NPCSC). The Basic Law requires that courts follow the NPCSC's interpretations where cases intersect with central government jurisdiction, although judgments previously rendered are not affected. On four occasions in the past and once in November this year, described below, the NPCSC issued interpretations of the Basic Law.

Political Prisoners and Detainees

There were no reports of political prisoners or detainees.

Civil Judicial Procedures and Remedies

There is an independent and impartial judiciary for civil matters and access to a court to bring lawsuits seeking damages for, or the cessation of, human rights violations. The SAR's courts continued to exercise a high degree of autonomy under the Basic Law, but many Hong Kong residents questioned the durability of this autonomy in the wake of the November NPCSC interpretation of the Basic Law that interrupted the judicial process in Hong Kong. Activists and other observers expressed concerns that the SAR government and central government had encroached on the judiciary's independence.

The Basic Law's Article 158 grants the NPCSC the power to interpret the Basic Law. On November 7, the NPCSC issued an interpretation on the Basic Law's language requiring all government officials to take an oath in order to enter office. The NPCSC issued its interpretation while the Court of First Instance was considering the Hong Kong Government's judicial review petitions against two proindependence legislators-elect. On November 9, Court of First Instance Justice Thomas Au ruled in favor of the government to disqualify the legislators-elect, noting he would have reached the same decision even if the NPCSC had not issued its interpretation. Legal scholars, the Hong Kong Bar Association, and the Law Society characterized the interpretation as unnecessary. They also voiced concern that the issuance of the interpretation might damage perceptions about the SAR's independent judiciary and the reputation of its courts, as well as the SAR's overall autonomy. The November 7 interpretation marked the first time the NPCSC had rendered an interpretation of the Basic Law while the matter in question was pending a judge's ruling and the second time it had done so in the absence of a request from Hong Kong authorities, which some legal experts viewed as inconsistent with the judicial reference process outlined in Article 158 of the Basic Law. Following issuance of the interpretation, hundreds of lawyers dressed in black and staged a silent protest against the NPCSC's failure to respect the autonomy of Hong Kong's judiciary.

Under Article 158, as originally enacted in 1997, the NPCSC's consults its Committee for the Basic Law, composed of six mainland and six Hong Kong members, before it issues an interpretation of the Basic Law. The Chief Executive, the LegCo president, and the chief justice nominate the Hong Kong members. Human rights and lawyers' organizations expressed concern that the lack of Hong Kong representation on the NPCSC (among the 175 current members, only one is a Hong Kong resident) and the limited power of the Basic Law Committee, could be used to limit the independence of the judiciary or degrade the Hong Kong courts' authority, as the NPCSC's decisions can supersede the Court of Final Appeal's power of final adjudication.

f. Arbitrary or Unlawful Interference with Privacy, Family, Home, or Correspondence

The law prohibits such actions, and the government generally respected these prohibitions.

Section 2. Respect for Civil Liberties, Including:

a. Freedom of Speech and Press

The law provides for freedom of speech and press, and the government generally respected these rights. An independent press, an effective judiciary, an unfettered internet, and a generally supportive government combined to promote freedom of speech and of the press on most matters. During the year, however, media groups complained about what they viewed as increasing challenges in this area. (For further detail, please see Press and Media Freedoms section below).

Freedom of Speech and Expression: There were no legal restrictions on the ability of individuals to criticize the government publicly or privately or to discuss matters of general public interest without reprisal. However, free speech advocates and educators voiced concern in August following the Education Secretary's public comments warning teachers who "advocate" Hong Kong independence on campus must "bear responsibility and consequences," including the loss of their teaching licenses. Subsequently, in September Chief Executive Leung said schools in Hong Kong had "no space to discuss independence." Educators, media outlets, and free speech advocates also voiced concern over comments made by Central Government officials based at Hong Kong's Central Government Liaison Office (CGLO). CGLO officials suggested publicly that discussion of Hong Kong's independence amounted to "a violation of laws in Hong Kong" and suggested it could be considered sedition and/or treason under Hong Kong's Crimes Ordinance if such speech was deemed to occur in the context of a "large-scale discussion in the hopes of gathering a large group to act together."

The Education Bureau made no formal changes to its policy following the Chief Executive's and Education Secretary's public comments. Members of the Professional Teachers Union reported there had been no changes to the guidance about how the union certifies its teachers.

Prospective candidates for public office reported Hong Kong's Electoral Affairs Commission implemented changes to its established procedures for filing legislative candidacy that limited free speech in the political arena. On July 12, the Electoral Affairs Commission instituted a new requirement that all LegCo candidates sign a pledge stating that Hong Kong is an "inalienable part" of China in order to run for office. Despite signing the required form and fulfilling other eligibility requirements, an Electoral Affairs Commission officer disqualified Hong Kong Indigenous convener Edward Leung and several other candidates for standing for election. The Electoral Affairs Commission said Leung's disqualification was due to Leung's proindependence comments earlier in the year, which the returning officer said was evidence that Leung was insincere in his loyalty pledge to the SAR. Leung's supporters voiced concern the new procedures infringed on freedom of speech and the right of Hong Kongers to stand for public office, rights guaranteed in the Basic Law.

On July 20, Zhang Xiaoming, the director of the CGLO, warned the Hong Kong government against allowing the LegCo elections in September to be used to promote "proindependence remarks and activities." Zhang suggested that allowing free speech on the matter violated the Basic Law and warned of "calamity" if proindependence views continued to spread in Hong Kong. While the CGLO Director has no legal standing, many local observers and free speech advocates said his public comments had a chilling effect on Hong Kong society.

Hong Kong residents also expressed concern about the potential implications of the November 7 NPCSC interpretation of Basic Law Article 104 on the SAR's free speech protections. The interpretation barred legislators-elect from taking office if they refused to take the oath, altered the wording of the oath, or failed to demonstrate sufficient "sincerity" or "solemnity" when taking the oath. Some observers and legal experts voiced concern that the NPCSC's interpretation could subject sitting legislators to legal sanctions if they "engage in conduct in breach of the oath" at any point in their respective terms. Prodemocracy advocates, particularly those who identify as "localists", expressed fears that the interpretation created a mechanism for the central government to exclude from office, or potentially evict from office, those who espoused or were suspected of harboring political views that the central government found objectionable. The interpretation stated that the requirements and preconditions contained within it applied to legislators-elect and all other public officers and candidates for public office referred to in Article 104. Some legal experts downplayed these concerns, noting the Basic Law's

Article 77 protects legislators from legal recourse stemming from any speeches they deliver in the normal course of their representative duties, while other legal experts have noted that the central government's powers over Hong Kong are not subject to any legal supervision, which manifests in the NPCSC's continued assertion of a power to interpret the Basic Law at its discretion.

Many in the media and civil society organizations further alleged the central government exerted indirect pressure on media organizations to mute criticism of its policy priorities in the SAR. They also voiced concern about increasing self-censorship among the local and regional press corps.

Press and Media Freedoms: In July the Hong Kong Journalists Association in its yearly report on press freedoms in Hong Kong said its Press Freedom Index indicators declined for the second straight year, from 38.9 to 38.2 points for journalists and from 48.4 to 47.4 for the general public. Nearly 85 percent of surveyed Hong Kong journalists thought that press freedom had worsened over the previous year. The report, which this year focused on increasing mainland influence on Hong Kong media outlets, cited as challenges continuing violence against journalists by police and protestors related to media coverage of local riots, lack of government transparency, the government's "questionable" policy on granting of television and radio licenses, and refusal to accredit online and student reporters (online reporters have since been granted accreditation). The Association called on the government to undertake a number of actions, including to "take a strong approach to protect the one country, two systems principle given the threats to Hong Kong's high degree of autonomy as promised in the Basic Law."

Violence and Harassment: No violent attacks on media-related personalities took place during the year.

Censorship or Content Restrictions: Reports of media self-censorship continued during the year. Most media outlets were owned by companies with business interests on the mainland, which led to claims that they were vulnerable to self-censorship, with editors deferring to the perceived concerns of publishers regarding their business interests. According to the Committee to Protect Journalists, more than half of Hong Kong's media owners held official roles in the PRC political system, either as delegates to the NPC or to the Chinese People's Political Consultative Conference.

Mainland companies and those with significant business dealings on the mainland reportedly boycotted advertising in the Next Media Group publications, known for its criticisms of the central government and the SAR government. Next Media Group's popular newspaper *Apple Daily* said it took special measures to circumvent regular hacking attacks, including the use of sophisticated email security software and asking its lawyers to use couriers instead of email. A private cybersecurity company that works with Next Media Group told Reuters in late 2015 that it had connected denial of service attacks against *Apple Daily* with professional cyber spying attacks that bore the hallmarks of a common source and suggested the hacker's apparent objectives matched the central government's.

Libel/Slander Laws: There were no reports the government or individual public figures used laws against libel, slander, defamation, or blasphemy to restrict public discussion.

National Security: There were no reports of restrictive media distribution to protect national security. Following the November 7 NPCSC interpretation of the Basic Law, Chief Executive Leung and some presumptive Chief Executive candidates indicated that the government would again consider national security legislation. No such legislation was under consideration by LegCo at year's end.

Internet Freedom

There were no government restrictions on access to the internet, although prodemocracy activists, legislators, lawyers, religious leaders, and protesters claimed central government authorities closely monitored their e-mails and internet use. The internet was widely available and used extensively.

There were reports of politically motivated cyberattacks against private persons and organizations.

In late 2015 the head of Hong Kong's Democratic Party said his party had repeatedly faced sophisticated cyberattacks on its website and against members' personal email accounts that appeared to originate from the central government. Before district council elections in November 2015, Reuters found that hackers had broken into at least 20 Gmail accounts belonging to the Democratic Party. Private cybersecurity company FireEye said attacks launched on Dropbox, in which specific victims were trapped into downloading infected files, targeted "precisely those whose networks Beijing would seek to monitor." The company said half its customers in Hong Kong, or two and a half times the global average, were attacked by government and professional hackers in the first half of 2015.

Academic Freedom and Cultural Events

There were some restrictions on academic freedom and cultural events. Some scholars suggested Hong Kong-based academics practiced self-censorship in their China-related work to preserve good relations and research and lecturing opportunities in the mainland.

In July, Hong Kong's Tiananmen Museum closed after two years of operation. The museum had been the only museum on PRC soil commemorating the 1989 Tiananmen Square massacre. According to CNN and Time, the Hong Kong Alliance, a prodemocracy group that operated the museum, said the closure was due to pressure from the owners' committee of the building, which made it difficult for the museum to operate by restricting visitor numbers, filing a lawsuit disputing the usage of the space as a museum, and forcing visitors to provide their names and personal information--a requirement that discouraged visitors from the mainland. The museum operators also cited high rent and other fundraising challenges, but said they kept the museum's exhibits and hoped to move to a new and bigger location in the future.

In August and September, the Education Secretary and the Chief Executive warned educators against the discussion of independence in schools. In September, Chief Executive Leung said schools in Hong Kong had "no space to discuss independence." However, at the year's end, the Education Bureau had made no policy changes in response to their comments, and members of the Professional Teachers' Union reported their union had made no changes to the regulations governing the accreditation of teachers and the issuance of teaching credentials. For further information, please see section 2.a.

On October 1, the national holiday marking the PRC's founding in 1949, students at eight universities in Hong Kong hung banners in support of Hong Kong independence. Media reports indicated that school officials promptly removed the banners.

Hong Kong-based international NGOs voiced concern about pro-Beijing media outlets' sustained criticism of their activities, which the newspapers characterized as interference by foreign forces. NGO staff members reported that these efforts to discredit their work in the SAR made it difficult for the groups to continue their existing partnerships with academic institutions and their public outreach. NGOs also voiced concern about the mainland's Foreign NGO Management Law, slated to enter into effect on January 1, 2017, noting the law would impose onerous restrictions on the ability to operate and implement social services delivery, advocacy work, and aid services. The law specifically defines Hong Kong-based organizations as covered by the law's requirements. In April the New York-based broadcaster New Tang Dynasty Television (NTD-TV) leased the Heung Yee Kuk Grand Theater in Hong Kong to hold a dance competition. NTD-TV received a notice from the theater in May stating that the Hong Kong Government requested the theater for the same date for use in association with the September Hong Kong LegCo election. The theater canceled NTD-TV's lease in June and offered a full refund for the contract, as well as assistance in identifying an alternative venue. NTD-TV then arranged to hold the competition at another venue, the government-subsidized Macpherson Stadium, in August, but the second venue also later revoked permission to use its premises. NTD-TV ultimately relocated the competition to Taiwan. NTD-TV is associated with the Falun Gong spiritual movement, which is banned in mainland China, but not in Hong Kong. Falun Gong advocates allege that the Hong Kong Government and the CGLO pressured these venues not to allow the dance competition to be held on their premises because of NTD-TV's association with Falun Gong.

b. Freedom of Peaceful Assembly and Association

Freedom of Assembly

The law provides for freedom of assembly, and the government generally respected this right. The police routinely issued the required "letter of no objection" for public meetings and demonstrations--including those critical of the SAR and central governments--and the overwhelming majority of protests occurred without serious incident. On June 4, tens of thousands of persons peacefully gathered without incident in Victoria Park to commemorate the 27th anniversary of the Tiananmen Square crackdown. The annual vigil and a smaller annual event in Macau were reportedly the only sanctioned events in China to commemorate the Tiananmen Square anniversary.

Figures vary for participation in the annual July 1 prodemocracy demonstration, held on the anniversary of the 1997 transfer of sovereignty over Hong Kong to the PRC. Police estimated 19,300 protesters; an independent polling organization estimated 29,000, and organizers claimed 110,000. Participants voiced concern over the Mighty Current booksellers' detentions, called for CE Leung to resign, supported a relaunch of Hong Kong's electoral reform process aimed at extending universal suffrage for all residents to vote in elections for the Chief Executive, encouraged abolition of LegCo's Functional Constituencies in favor of directly electing all legislators; and demanded democratic amendments to the Basic Law. Police deployed hundreds of officers, and did not interfere with the legally permitted rally.

Government statistics indicated police arrested 125 persons in connection with public order events in the first half of last year; statistics were not yet available for 2016.

Freedom of Association

The law provides for freedom of association, and the government generally respected it.

c. Freedom of Religion

See the Department of State's *International Religious Freedom Report* at www.state.gov/religiousfreedomreport/.

d. Freedom of Movement, Internally Displaced Persons, Protection of Refugees, and Stateless Persons

The law provides for freedom of internal movement, foreign travel, emigration, and repatriation and the government generally respected these rights, with some prominent exceptions.

Under the "one country, two systems" framework, the SAR continued to administer its own immigration and entry policies and make determinations regarding claims under the UN Convention against Torture (CAT) independently. Hong Kong is not a signatory to the 1951 UN Refugee Convention or the 1969 Protocol. As such, the SAR only accepts asylum claims on the basis of torture in a claimant's home country. The most recently available government statistics indicated that there were over 11,000 nonrefoulement claims, including those based on claims under the CAT, pending Immigration Department processing. Applicants and activists continued to complain about the slow processing of claims and limited government subsidies available to applicants. Activists and refugee rights groups also voiced concerns about the very low rate of approved claims (0.6

percent for a recent 15 month period), suggesting the government's bar for approving claims of torture was far higher than other developed jurisdictions.

The government cooperated with the Office of the UN High Commissioner for Refugees (UNHCR) and the International Organization for Migration as well as other humanitarian organizations in providing protection and assistance to internally displaced persons, refugees, returning refugees, asylum seekers, stateless persons, or other persons of concern.

There continued to be claims that the Immigration Department refused entry to a small number of persons traveling to the SAR for political reasons that did not appear to contravene the law. The Immigration Department, as a matter of policy, declined to comment on individual cases. Activists, some legislators, and other observers contended that the refusals, usually of persons holding views critical of the central government, were made at the behest of PRC authorities. The Security Bureau maintained that the Immigration Department exchanged information with other immigration authorities, including on the mainland, but made its decisions independently.

Foreign Travel: Most residents easily obtained travel documents from the SAR government; however, central government authorities did not permit some human rights activists, student protesters, and prodemocracy legislators to visit mainland China. Some of the students who participated in the protest movement in the fall of 2014 alleged the central government security agencies surveilled the protests and blacklisted them.

The central government took steps to restrict the foreign travel of prominent prodemocracy leaders, according to civil society representatives. In October, Thai immigration authorities blocked democracy activist Joshua Wong from entering the country to speak at Bangkok's Chulalongkorn University and detained him at the airport for 12 hours without explanation. Wong was to attend an event to commemorate the 40th anniversary of a massacre on the campus of Bangkok's Thammaset University. Upon his return to Hong Kong, Wong told the press he believed Thai authorities were responding to pressure from the central government. A senior immigration official told a Thai newspaper that Wong was denied entry in response to a request from the PRC government. The Thai organizer who invited Wong to speak at the university also said Thai police had informed him that they had received a letter about Wong from PRC authorities.

<u>Emigration and Repatriation</u>: Government policy was to repatriate undocumented migrants who arrived from mainland China, and authorities did not consider them for refugee status.

The government did not recognize the Taiwan passport as valid for visa endorsement purposes, although convenient mechanisms existed for Taiwan passport holders to visit. As of 2013 most Taiwan visitors have been able to register online and stay for one month if they hold a mainland travel permit.

Protection of Refugees

<u>Access to Asylum</u>: The SAR has a policy of not granting asylum or refugee status and has no temporary protection policy. The government's practice was to refer refugee and asylum claimants to a lawyer or to UNHCR. Persons wishing to file a claim cannot do so while they have legally entered the SAR, and must instead wait until they have overstayed the terms of their entry before they can file such a claim.

<u>Refoulement</u>: The government's Unified Screening Mechanism, introduced last year, consolidated the processing of claims based on risk of return to persecution, torture, or cruel, inhuman, or degrading treatment or punishment. Claimants continued to receive publicly funded legal assistance, including translation services, as well as small living subsidies. The children of refugee claimants can usually attend Hong Kong's public schools, if the Director of Immigration deems adjudication of a claim will take several months. The number of substantiated cases of torture and nonrefoulement is less than one percent of the total determinations made since 2009. According to the HKSAR Immigration Department, between the commencement of the enhanced administrative mechanism in late 2009 and September 2016, determinations were made in 10,172 torture/nonrefoulement claims, among which only 65 were substantiated.

<u>Employment</u>: The government defines CAT claimants and asylum seekers as illegal immigrants or "overstayers" in the SAR, and as such they have no legal right to work in the SAR while claims are under review. Those granted either refugee status by UNHCR or relief from removal under the CAT could work only with approval from the director of immigration. They were also ineligible for training by either the Employees Retraining Board or the Vocational Training Council.

Section 3. Freedom to Participate in the Political Process

The Basic Law limits the ability of residents to change their government through free and fair elections. Article 45 of the Basic Law establishes as the "ultimate aim" direct election of the chief executive through "universal suffrage upon nomination by a broadly representative nominating committee in accordance with democratic procedures." Since 2007 the people of Hong Kong, the SAR government, and the PRC central government have vigorously debated the nature, scope, and pace of democratic and electoral reforms.

Voters directly elect 40 of LegCo's 70 seats by secret ballot. Thirty-five seats are designated as "geographic constituencies" (GCs) and 35 as "functional constituencies" (FCs). All 35 GCs are directly elected, while only five of the FCs are directly elected. The remaining 30 FC seats are selected by a subset of voters from FCs representing various economic and social sectors, which typically hold proestablishment views. Under this structure a limited number of individuals and institutions were able to control multiple votes for LegCo members. In 2016, the constituencies that elected these 30 FC LegCo seats consisted of 232,498 registered individual and institutional voters, of which some 172,820 voted, according to the SAR's election affairs office statistics. The five FC seats in the district council sector, known as "super seats" were directly elected by the approximately five million registered voters who were not otherwise represented in another FC and therefore represented larger constituencies than any other seats in LegCo. The government has previously acknowledged the method of selecting FC legislators did not conform to the principle of universal suffrage, but it took no steps to eliminate the FCs in 2016.

In addition to strong showings from traditional prodemocracy parties, seven self-proclaimed "localists" won seats for the first time. The "localists" represent a range of political views, with campaign platforms variously focused on a referendum on self-determination after 2047; Hong Kong-first-focused policies; reforms for land development policies; and proindependence. The platform for the top vote-getter for the geographical constituency with the largest electorate, Chu Hoi-dick, touted self-determination in addition to land reform and environmental concerns. The "localists" in some cases won legislative seats over more traditional prodemocracy parties, leading to a wide range of views expressed within the LegCo.

Under the Basic Law, LegCo members may not introduce bills that affect public expenditure, the political structure, or government policy; only the government may introduce these types of bills. The SAR sends 36 deputies to the mainland's

NPC and had approximately 250 delegates in the Chinese People's Political Consultative Conference--bodies that operate under the direction of the CCP and do not exercise legislative independence. The approval of the CE, two-thirds of LegCo, and two-thirds of the SAR's delegates to the NPC are required to place an amendment to the Basic Law on the agenda of the NPC, which has the sole power to amend the Basic Law.

Voters directly elected all 431 of Hong Kong's district council seats in November 2015 following the government's elimination of appointed district council seats. Previously, the CE used his authority to appoint 68 of the 534 members of the district councils, the SAR's most grassroots-level elected bodies.

Elections and Political Participation

Recent Elections: In 2012, in a process widely criticized as undemocratic, the 1,193-member CE Election Committee, dominated by proestablishment electors and their allies, selected C.Y. Leung to be the SAR's chief executive. Leung received 689 votes. The PRC's State Council formally appointed him, and then President Hu Jintao swore in Leung.

The next chief executive election is scheduled for March 2017 under an electoral process identical to the 2012 process, because the LegCo rejected an electoral reform package in June 2015 that prodemocracy legislators considered insufficiently democratic on the grounds that it did not allow voters directly to nominate the candidates for chief executive. On December 11, representatives of various commercial sectors, professions, religious organizations, and social service providers, as well as political representatives, elected the 1,194 electors who will cast ballots in the next chief executive election. Residents voiced concern that these small-circle elections were open to participation by a very small number (230,000) of the SAR's 7.5 million residents. Additionally, while the 2016 Election Committee elections saw historically high turnout of 46 percent and a record number of contested seats across industrial, professional, grassroots, and political sectors, local political observers noted 300 members--approximately 25 percent--of the committee were elected without a poll or other transparent election process to represent 12 uncontested subsectors and one sub-subsector.

In September SAR residents elected representatives to the 70-member LegCo. The election, which saw record high turnout of 2.2 million voters, or over 58 percent, was considered generally free and fair according to the standards established in the Basic Law. The government acknowledged election observers and other residents had filed approximately 1,200 petitions about election misconduct with the Elections Affairs Committee following the conclusion of the LegCo election. Pro-PRC and proestablishment candidates won 40 of 70 LegCo seats, while prodemocracy candidates won 30, an increase over the 27 the opposition camp held from 2012 to 2016.

In July, for the first time the government announced all LegCo candidates would have to sign a Confirmation Form pledging their allegiance to the SAR and their intent to uphold the Basic Law, including three provisions that stated Hong Kong is an inalienable part of the PRC. Legal scholars and prodemocracy activists criticized the government's use of the Confirmation Form, noting the LegCo had not approved this change to the election procedures or the requirements for candidates to stand for legislative office. In August the government disqualified proindependence LegCo candidate Edward Leung, of the Hong Kong Indigenous party, from running in the election in the New Territories East district. An elections officer refused Leung's candidacy, even though Leung had signed the Confirmation Form and said he would drop his proindependence stance. Leung and another candidate filed judicial review applications charging that the use of the Confirmation Form was not in accordance with the SAR's laws. Leung also filed an elections petition in September alleging his disqualification from the race was unlawful.

Some observers expressed concern that the interpretation could restrict the right to stand for office guaranteed in Article 26 of the Basic Law for those who espouse proindependence views, and possibly for those who support self-determination as well. At the end of the year, the Hong Kong high court had disqualified two proindependence legislators-elect, Yau Wai-ching and Sixtus Leung, from taking office. The September election of proindependence legislators followed a July poll of public opinion conducted by the Chinese University of Hong Kong that found that while only 4 percent of respondents thought independence was possible for Hong Kong, 17 percent of them, including 39 percent of respondents aged 15 to 24, supported independence when the current political arrangement expires in 2047.

At a press conference announcing the NPCSC interpretation, NPCSC Legal Committee Chair Li Fei suggested that support for self-determination would be treated the same as promoting independence, and could thus disqualify legislators under the new interpretation. On December 2, Chief Executive Leung and Secretary for Justice Yuen filed a legal challenge to the legitimacy of four other opposition legislators--veteran activist "Long Hair" Leung Kwok-hung, former Occupy Central student leader Nathan Law, lecturer Lau Siu-lai, and university professor Edward Yiu--over the manner in which they took their oaths. The courts accepted the government's judicial review application on December 15, and initial hearings for the cases are expected to be held in February 2017. Support for "localist" platforms, including self-determination (generally understood to refer to a referendum on Hong Kong's status in 2047) was a key component of several elected legislators' platforms, including those of Law and Lau.

The Independent Commission against Corruption (ICAC) was estimated to have received well over 200 complaints concerning alleged breaches of provisions under the Elections (Corrupt and Illegal Conduct) Ordinance. Media reported the complaints included allegations of fraudulently registering voters without their consent, bribing voters, voting after giving false or misleading information to an elections officer, incurring election expenses by persons other than the candidate or his agent, publishing false or misleading statements about a candidate, publishing election advertisements that did not meet certain requirements, failing to file election returns, and providing others with refreshments and entertainment at elections.

Political Parties and Political Participation: Pandemocratic parties faced a number of institutional challenges, which hampered them from securing a majority of the seats in the LegCo or having one of their members become CE. Of LegCo's 70 seats, 30 were elected by FCs, most of whom are supportive of the central government; representatives from 12 of these constituencies ran unopposed, while over 150 parties contested the SAR's 35 GC seats. The law does not permit tax-exempt contributions to political parties. The voting process helped ensure that proestablishment allies controlled a majority of seats in LegCo. Additionally, the central government and its business supporters provided generous financial resources to parties that supported the central government's political agenda in the SAR, ensuring that these organizations would control the levers of government and senior positions. According to local press reports, several political groups voiced concern that the Central Government Liaison Office (CGLO) interfered with legislative campaigns, lobbying for pro-Beijing candidates and threatening or harassing others. In August, Liberal Party candidate Ken Chow suspended his campaign for a LegCo seat, alleging CGLO affiliates had harassed him and threatened the safety of his family. At year's end, the ICAC, the Liberal Party, and the HKG had undertaken investigations into Chow's allegations. Chow subsequently quit the Liberal Party.

Participation of Women and Minorities: Five of the 30 members of the Executive Council (cabinet-level secretaries and "nonofficial" councilors who advise the CE) were women. Eleven of the 40 directly-elected LegCo members were women, and a woman held one of the 35 FC seats. Fourteen of the 45 most senior government officials (secretaries, undersecretaries, and permanent secretaries) were women.

There is no legal restriction against non-Chinese running for electoral office, serving as electoral monitors, or participating in the civil service, although most elected or senior appointed positions require that the officeholder have a legal right of abode only in the SAR. There were no members of ethnic minorities in the LegCo. The government regarded ethnic origin as irrelevant to civil service appointment and did not require applicants to declare their ethnicity or race in their applications for government jobs. Some observers criticized this practice as preventing the government from monitoring hiring and promotion rates for individuals who were not ethnically Chinese. In March, citing underrepresentation of ethnic minorities in the government, a local foundation published a list of 16 ethnic minority candidates who had relevant experience and Cantonese language, encouraging the government to appoint these candidates to serve on government advisory committees.

Section 4. Corruption and Lack of Transparency in Government

The law provides criminal penalties for official corruption, and the government generally implemented it effectively. The SAR continued to be viewed as relatively uncorrupt.

Corruption: In July controversy erupted over the independence and impartiality of the ICAC after a senior official leading a corruption investigation of Chief Executive Leung was mysteriously demoted. Prior to the demotion, Rebecca Li, who led the ICAC operations department, had a distinguished career spanning three decades. In 2015, she became the agency's most senior career official, a first for a woman. Li's department was responsible for conducting an investigation into whether Mr. Leung properly disclosed U.S. $6.4 million in payments he received from an Australian company that does business with the city. Li resigned following the demotion. Her sudden departure reportedly led one of her top investigators to resign in protest, and ICAC employees collectively refused to attend the annual staff dinner in protest and forced its cancellation. ICAC had not yet provided its perspective by year's end.

In October the prosecution in an existing case charging former chief executive Donald Tsang with two counts of misconduct in public office in connection with a below-market lease and hiring of an architect for a luxury apartment in Shenzhen added an additional bribery charge related to the redecoration of the penthouse. Together, the charges carry a maximum HK$500,000 fine and seven years imprisonment. Tsang remained free on bail while the cases proceeded; his trial reopened in January 2017.

Financial Disclosure: The SAR requires the 27 most senior civil service officials to declare their financial investments annually and the approximately 3,100 senior working-level officials to do so biennially. Policy bureaus may impose additional reporting requirements for positions seen as having a greater risk of conflict of interest. The Civil Service Bureau monitors and verifies disclosures, which are available to the public. There are criminal and administrative sanctions for noncompliance.

Public Access to Information: There is no freedom of information law. An administrative code on access to information serves as the framework for the provision of information by government bureaus and departments and the ICAC.

Under the code authorities may refuse to disclose information if doing so would cause or risk causing harm or prejudice in several broad areas: national security and foreign affairs (which are reserved to the central government); immigration issues; judicial and law enforcement issues; direct risks to individuals; damage to the environment; improper gain or advantage; management of the economy; management and operation of the public service; internal discussion and advice; public employment and public appointments; research, statistics, and analysis; third-party information; business affairs; premature requests; and information on which legal restrictions apply. Political inconvenience or the potential for embarrassment were not justifiable bases for withholding information.

Section 5. Governmental Attitude Regarding International and Nongovernmental Investigation of Alleged Violations of Human Rights

A wide variety of domestic and international human rights groups generally operated without government restriction, investigating and publishing their findings on human rights cases. Government officials generally were cooperative and responsive to their views. Prominent human rights activists critical of the central government also operated freely and maintained permanent resident status in the SAR.

Government Human Rights Bodies: There is an Office of the Ombudsman and an Equal Opportunities Commission (EOC). The government recruits commissioners to represent both offices through a professional search committee, which solicits applications and vets candidates. Commissioners were independent in their operations. Both organizations operated without interference from the government and published critical findings in their areas of responsibility. In January the EOC, under the supervision of Commissioner Dr. York Chow, published a list of 77 recommendations for how to update the SAR's existing antidiscrimination legislation to better protect Hong Kong's lesbian, gay, bisexual, transgender, and intersex (LGBTI) individuals, improve access to public and commercial buildings for persons with disabilities, and other issues within the EOC's responsibility. In March, Lingnan University professor Alfred Chan replaced Chow as EOC Commissioner; Chan continues to serve the EOC as an advocate for LGBTI rights, the ethnic minority community, and persons with disabilities.

Section 6. Discrimination, Societal Abuses, and Trafficking in Persons

Women

Rape and Domestic Violence: The law criminalizes rape, including spousal rape, and police enforced the law effectively. Activists voiced concerns that rape was underreported, especially within the ethnic minority community, but acknowledged the police responded appropriately in reported cases.

The government regarded domestic violence against women as a serious concern and took measures to prevent and prosecute offenses. The law allows victims to seek a three-month injunction, extendable to six months, against an abuser. Although the law does not criminalize domestic violence directly, abusers may be liable for criminal charges under other ordinances. The government effectively enforced the law and prosecuted violators, but sentences typically consisted only of injunctions or restraining orders.

The law covers molestation between married couples, homosexual and heterosexual cohabitants, former spouses or cohabitants, and immediate and extended family members. It protects victims under age 18, allowing them to apply for an injunction in their own right, with the assistance of an adult guardian, against molestation by their parents, siblings, and specified immediate and extended family members. The law also empowers the court to require that the abuser attend an antiviolence program. In cases in which the abuser caused bodily harm, the court may attach an authorization of arrest to an existing injunction and extend both injunctions and authorizations for arrest to two years.

The government maintained programs that provided intervention, counseling, and assistance to domestic violence victims and batterers. The government continued its public information campaign to strengthen families and to prevent violence.

Activists reported domestic violence was more prevalent against ethnic minority women.

Sexual Harassment: The law prohibits sexual harassment or discrimination on the basis of sex, marital status, and pregnancy. The law applies to both men and women, and police enforced the law effectively.

Reproductive Rights: Couples and individuals have the right to decide the number, spacing, and timing of children; manage their reproductive health; and have access to the information and means to do so, free from discrimination, coercion, or violence.

Discrimination: Women enjoy the same legal status and rights as men. The SAR's sexual discrimination ordinance prohibits discrimination on the grounds of sex or pregnancy status, and the government generally enforced this antidiscrimination law.

According to gender-rights activists and public policy analysts, while the law treats men and women equally in terms of property rights in divorce settlements and inheritance matters, women faced discrimination in employment, salary, welfare, inheritance, and promotion.

The law authorizes the EOC to work towards the elimination of discrimination and harassment as well as to promote equal opportunity between men and women. A Women's Commission served as an advisory body for policies related to women, and a number of NGOs were active in raising problems of societal attitudes and discrimination against women.

Children

Birth Registration: All Chinese nationals born in the SAR, on the PRC mainland, or abroad to parents of whom at least one is a PRC-national Hong Kong permanent resident acquire both PRC citizenship and Hong Kong permanent residence, the latter allowing the right of abode in the SAR. Children born in the SAR to non-Chinese parents, at least one of whom is a Hong Kong permanent resident, acquire SAR permanent residence and qualify to apply for naturalization as PRC citizens. Registration of all such statuses was routine.

Child Abuse: The law mandates protection for victims of child abuse (battery, assault, neglect, abandonment, and sexual exploitation), and the government enforced the law. The law allows for the prosecution of certain sexual offenses, including against minors, committed outside the territory of the SAR.

The government provided parent-education programs through its maternal and child health centers, public education programs, clinical psychologists for its clinical psychology units, and social workers for its family and child protective services units. Police maintained a child abuse investigation unit and in collaboration with the Social Welfare Department ran a child witness support program. A law on child-care centers helped prevent unsuitable persons from providing childcare services.

Early and Forced Marriage: The legal minimum age of marriage is 16, and parents' written consent is required for marriage before the age of 21. There was no evidence of early or forced marriage in the SAR.

Sexual Exploitation of Children: There were reports of girls under the age of 18 from some countries in Asia being subjected to sex trafficking in the SAR.

The legal age of consent is 16. Under the law a person having "unlawful sexual intercourse" with a victim under 16 is subject to five years' imprisonment, while having unlawful sexual intercourse with a victim under 13 carries a sentence of life imprisonment.

The law makes it an offense to possess, produce, copy, import, or export pornography involving a child under the age of 18 or to publish or cause to be published any advertisement that conveys or is likely to be understood as conveying the message that a person has published, publishes, or intends to publish any child pornography. Authorities generally enforced the law. The penalty for creation, publication, or advertisement of child pornography is eight years' imprisonment, while possession carries a penalty of five years' imprisonment.

<u>International Child Abductions</u>: The SAR is a party to the 1980 Hague Convention on the Civil Aspects of International Child Abduction. See the Department of State's *Annual Report on International Parental Child Abduction* at travel.state.gov/content/childabduction/en/legal/compliance.html.

Anti-Semitism

The Jewish community numbered 5,000 to 6,000 persons and reported few acts of anti-Semitism during the year. There were concerns within the Jewish community about some religious rhetoric heard from the otherwise moderate Muslim community.

Trafficking in Persons

See the Department of State's *Trafficking in Persons Report* at www.state.gov/j/tip/rls/tiprpt/.

Persons with Disabilities

The law prohibits discrimination against persons with physical, sensory, intellectual, and mental disabilities in employment, education, access to health care, air travel and other transportation, and the provision of other state services, including access to the judicial system and the government generally enforced these provisions. The government generally implemented laws and programs to ensure that persons with disabilities have access to buildings, information, and communications, although there were reports of some restrictions.

The Disability Discrimination Ordinance states that children with special education needs must have equal opportunity in accessing education. It is against the law for a school to discriminate against a student with a disability. According to the government, students with significant or multiple disabilities are, with parental consent, placed in special segregated schools, while students with less significant disabilities are enrolled in mainstream schools. There were occasional media reports about alleged abuses in education and mental health facilities; the most recent court case involving such abuses was in 2011.

The SAR implemented a range of legislative, administrative, and other measures to enhance the rights of persons with disabilities. Some human rights groups reported that the SAR's Disability Discrimination Ordinance was too limited and did not oblige the government to promote equal opportunities.

The Social Welfare Department provided training and vocational rehabilitation services to assist persons with disabilities, offered subsidized resident-care services for persons considered unable to live independently and offered places for preschool services to children with disabilities, and provided community support services for persons with mental disabilities, their families, and other local residents.

Persons with disabilities filed legal cases indicating instances of discrimination against persons with disabilities persisted in employment, education, and the provision of some public services. The law calls for improved building access and sanctions against those who discriminate. Access to public buildings (including public schools) and transportation remained a serious problem for persons with disabilities.

Some persons with disabilities protested that the government discriminated against them with respect to social security assistance.

According to the EOC, the SAR lagged in providing equal opportunities for students with disabilities, despite having operated an integrated education policy since 1997.

National/Racial/Ethnic Minorities

Although 94 percent ethnic Chinese, Hong Kong is a multi-ethnic society with persons from a number of ethnic groups recognized as permanent residents with full rights under the law. The law prohibits discrimination, and the EOC oversees implementation and enforcement of the law. The EOC maintained a hotline for inquiries and complaints concerning racial discrimination. The EOC's code of practice (along with selected other EOC materials) was available in Hindi, Thai, Urdu, Nepali, Indonesian, and Tagalog, in addition to Chinese and English.

The government has a policy to integrate non-Chinese students into the SAR's schools and provided a special grant for some schools to develop their own programs, share best practices with other schools, develop supplementary curriculum materials, and set up Chinese-language support centers to provide after-school programs. Activists and scholars noted that programs encouraging predominantly Chinese schools to welcome minority students backfired, turning certain schools into "segregated institutions." These schools reportedly did not teach Chinese to the non-ethnic Chinese students. Students who did not learn Chinese had significant difficulty entering university and the labor market, according to government and NGO reports.

Activists continued to express concern that there was no formal government-sponsored course to prepare students for the General Certificate for Secondary Education examination in Chinese, a passing grade from which is required for most civil service employment. The government provided funds to subsidize the cost of these examinations. The government began accepting alternate credentials for Hong Kong students to enter the SAR's universities, though scholars assessed ethnic minority students faced a tough choice between either preparing for the General Certificate examination, which would enable entry into many civil service jobs, or preparing for alternate tests, which might enable entry into the SAR's universities.

Activists and the government disputed whether new immigrants from the mainland should be considered as a population of concern under antidiscrimination laws. While concerns were raised that new immigrants do not qualify to receive social welfare benefits until they have resided in the SAR for seven years, the courts upheld this legal standard. Such immigrants could apply on a case-specific basis for assistance.

Acts of Violence, Discrimination, and Other Abuses based on Sexual Orientation and Gender Identity

No laws criminalize consensual same-sex sexual activity. While the SAR has laws that ban discrimination on the grounds of race, sex, disability, and family status, no law prohibits companies or individuals from discriminating on grounds of sexual orientation or gender identity; there are also no laws that specifically aid in the prosecution of bias-motivated crimes against members of the LGBTI community.

The government claimed public education and existing civil and criminal laws were sufficient to protect the rights of the LGBTI community and that legislation was not necessary. A small community of religious organizations continued to lobby the government and campaign actively to prevent the SAR's recognition of same-sex marriage. LGBTI professionals are permitted to bring foreign partners to the SAR only on a "prolonged visitor visa." Successful applicants, however, cannot work, obtain an identification card, or qualify for permanent residency.

LGBTI persons were able to arrange large scale activities, including pride marches and other community events.

Section 7. Worker Rights

a. Freedom of Association and the Right to Collective Bargaining

The law provides for the right of workers to form and join independent unions without previous authorization or excessive requirements and to conduct legal strikes, but it does not protect the right to collective bargaining or obligate employers to bargain. Trade unions claimed the law allows employers simply to refuse to bargain. The law explicitly prohibits civil servants from bargaining collectively; the International Labor Organization (ILO) advised this restriction was too broad and not in line with international standards.

Trade unions must register with the government's Registry of Trade Unions and must have a minimum membership of seven persons for registration. Workers were not prevented from unionizing, but only Hong Kong residents could join unions or serve as union officers. The law allows the use of union funds for political purposes, provided a union has the authorization of the majority of its voting members at a general meeting.

The law provides for the right to strike, although there are some restrictions on this right for civil servants. The Commissioner of police has broad authority to control and direct public gatherings in the interest of national security or public safety. According to the Employment Ordinance, an employer cannot fire, penalize, or discriminate against an employee who exercises his or her union rights and cannot prevent or deter the employee from exercising such rights. Under the Employment Ordinance, an employee unreasonably and unlawfully dismissed (including on the grounds of the employee exercising trade union rights) is entitled to reinstatement or reengagement, subject to mutual consent of the employer and the employee, or compensation up to a maximum of HK$150,000 ($19,300) for unreasonable and unlawful dismissal.

Penalties for violations of laws providing for freedom of association and collective bargaining laws included fines payable to the government as well as legal damages paid to workers and were sufficient to deter violations. Under the Employment Ordinance, employers who violated antiunion laws were liable to a fine of HK$100,000 ($13,000). Administrative and judicial procedures were not subject to lengthy delays.

The government effectively enforced the law. The Workplace Consultation Promotion Division in the Labor Department facilitated communication, consultation, and voluntary negotiation between employers and employees. Tripartite committees for each of the nine sectors of the economy included representatives from some trade unions, employers, and the Labor Department. During a labor dispute, the Labor Relations Division of the Labor Department facilitates conciliation so that the dispute can be settled with minimum friction and disruption.

Worker organizations were independent of the government and political parties. Prodemocracy labor activists alleged, however, that only progovernment unions were able to participate substantively in the tripartite process, while the prodemocracy Hong Kong Confederation of Trade Unions was consistently excluded. Trade Unions are prohibited from using funds for "political purposes."

Although there is no legislative prohibition against strikes and the right and freedom to strike are enshrined in the Basic Law, most workers had to sign employment contracts that typically stated walking off the job was a breach of contract and could lead to summary dismissal, though there were no incidents in 2016 that tested this legal contradiction. Various sections of the Employment Ordinance prohibit firing an employee for striking and void any section of an employment contract that would punish a worker for striking. As in past years, approximately 5,000 participated in the annual May 1 Labor Day march calling for standard working hours and a universal pension program. According to the government, there were no reports that employers fired workers for participating in a strike last year. The government reported that as of September last year, two strikes involving 106 workers had occurred. Activists claimed more strikes took place but that the government did not want to tarnish the SAR's business-friendly image by acknowledging them.

b. Prohibition of Forced or Compulsory Labor

The law does not prohibit all forms of forced or compulsory labor, nor do laws specifically criminalize forced labor. Hong Kong does not have a specific law explicitly banning labor trafficking. Instead, the SAR uses its Employment and Theft Ordinances to prosecute labor violations and related offenses.

NGOs voiced concerns some migrant workers faced high levels of indebtedness assumed as part of the recruitment process, creating a risk they could fall victim to debt bondage. The SAR allows for the collection of placement fees up to 10 percent of the first month's wages, but some recruitment firms required large up-front fees in the country of origin that workers struggled to repay even after arriving and working in Hong Kong for some time. Some locally licensed employment agencies were suspected of colluding with agencies in the Philippines and Indonesia to profit from a debt scheme, and some local agencies illegally confiscated the passports, employment contracts, and automatic teller machine cards of domestic workers and withheld them until their debt had been repaid. The government conveyed its concerns about these cases to a number of foreign missions.

There also were reports that some employers illegally forbade domestic workers from leaving the residence of work for non-work-related reasons, effectively preventing them from reporting exploitation to authorities. SAR authorities claimed they encouraged aggrieved workers to lodge complaints and make use of government conciliation services, as well as actively pursued reports of any labor violations.

Also see the Department of State's *Trafficking in Persons Report* at www.state.gov/j/tip/rls/tiprpt/.

c. Prohibition of Child Labor and Minimum Age for Employment

Regulations prohibit employment of children under age 15 in any industrial establishment. Other regulations limit work hours in the manufacturing sector for persons ages 15-17 to eight hours per day and 48 hours per week between 7 a.m. and 7 p.m. The law prohibits overtime in industrial establishments with employment in dangerous trades for persons under the age of 18.

Children aged 13-14 may work in certain nonindustrial establishments, subject to conditions aimed at ensuring a minimum of nine years of education and protection of their safety, health, and welfare.

The Labor Department effectively enforced these laws and regularly inspected workplaces to enforce compliance with the regulations. Penalties for violations of child labor laws include fines and legal damages up to HK$50,000 ($6,500) and were sufficient to deter violations. In the first eight months of the year, the Labor Department detected no violations of child labor regulations.

There were some reports that girls from some countries in Asia were subjected to commercial sexual exploitation (see section 6, Children).

d. Discrimination with respect to Employment and Occupation

The law and regulations prohibit employment discrimination on the grounds of race or ethnicity, disability, family status (marital status and/or pregnancy), or sex. The law stipulates employers must prove that proficiency in a particular language is a justifiable job requirement if they reject a candidate on these grounds. Regulations do not prohibit employment discrimination on the grounds of color, religion, political opinion, national origin or citizenship, sexual orientation and/or gender identity, HIV-positive status or other communicable diseases, or social status.

The government generally enforced these laws and regulations. In cases in which employment discrimination occurred, the SAR's courts had broad powers to levy penalties on those who violated these laws and regulations. Penalties included ordering reinstatement of employees as well as the awarding of damages for loss or emotional damages. These penalties were sufficient to deter violations.

Women reported they faced discrimination in employment, salary, welfare, inheritance, and promotion, and some victims filed lawsuits on these grounds. NGOs assessed gender discrimination was more widespread, but many women preferred not to file discrimination cases. Women reportedly formed the majority of the working poor and those who fell outside the protection of labor laws. Instances of discrimination against persons with disabilities persisted in employment and access. The government estimated approximately 81,000 persons with disabilities were economically active throughout the SAR, of whom 76,200 were employed. LGBTI persons reported discrimination in finding and keeping employment if they disclosed their sexual orientation or sexual identity.

Human rights activists and local scholars continued to raise concerns about job prospects for minority students, who are more likely to hold low-paying, low-skilled jobs and earn below-average wages. Academics assessed the lack of Chinese language skills were the greatest barriers to employment. Minority group leaders and activists reported government requirements for all job applicants to speak Chinese kept nonnative Chinese speakers out of civil service and law enforcement positions. The police force reportedly employed 100 non-ethnic-Chinese constables as of the beginning of the year.

e. Acceptable Conditions of Work

The statutory minimum hourly wage was readjusted last year to HK$32.50 ($4.18). On October 1, the SAR increased domestic workers' minimum monthly wage from HK$4,210 ($542) to HK$4,310 ($555) and increased their minimum monthly food allowance from HK$995 ($128) to HK$1,037 ($134).

The official poverty line was half of the median monthly household income before tax and welfare transfers, based on household size. For a one-person household, the poverty line was set at HK$3,600 ($463), for a two-person household HK$7,700 ($990), for a three-person household HK$11,500 ($1,480), and so on. According to this definition, more than 1.3 million persons (in a population of approximately 7.2 million) were living in poverty.

There is no law concerning working hours, paid weekly rest, rest breaks, or compulsory overtime for most employees. For certain groups and occupations, such as security guards and certain categories of drivers, there are regulations and guidelines on working hours and rest breaks. The law stipulates that employees are entitled to 12 days of statutory holidays and employers must not make payment in lieu of granting holidays. Local union groups and the government continued to debate standard working hours legislation, differing in whether the weekly standard should be set at 40, 44, or 48 hours. In the absence of such legislation, labor rights groups reported most Hong Kong residents work approximately 56 hours a week.

The government's Standard Employment Contract requires employers to provide foreign domestic workers with housing, worker's compensation insurance, travel allowances, and food or a food allowance in addition to the monthly minimum wage of approximately U.S. $542, which together provided a decent standard of living. In its explanation of why live-in domestic workers (both local and foreign) would not be covered by the statutory minimum wage, the government explained "the distinctive working pattern--round-the-clock presence, provision of service-on-demand, and the multifarious domestic duties expected of live-in domestic workers--made it impossible to ascertain the actual hours worked so as to determine the wages to be paid."

Foreign domestic workers could be deported if dismissed. After leaving one employer, workers have two weeks to secure new employment before they must leave the SAR. Activists contended this restriction left workers vulnerable to abuse by employers. Workers who pursued complaints through legal channels could be granted leave to remain in the SAR but could not work, leaving them either to live from savings or depend on charitable assistance. The government contended the "two-week rule" was necessary to maintain effective immigration control and prevent migrant workers from overstaying and taking unauthorized work.

The government enforced the law. The Labor Tribunal received employment cases and convicted employers in disputes involving foreign domestic workers, most of which the government said were related to nonpayment or underpayment of wages and wrongful dismissal. Domestic workers could also be subject to physical and verbal abuse, poor living and working conditions, and limitations on freedom of movement.

In late December a High Court judge ruled that the government failed to protect adequately the human rights and safety of a Pakistani man trafficked to Hong Kong and forced into unpaid labor for several years. At year's end, the government had not indicated if it planned to file an appeal of the case. The government stated the rules on labor protections and time off cover local and migrant workers.

Laws exist to provide for health and safety of workers in the workplace. Workers may remove themselves from situations that endanger health or safety without jeopardy to their employment. No laws restrict work during typhoon or rainstorm warnings. The Labor Department issued a "code of practice" on work arrangements in times of severe weather, which includes a recommendation that employers require only essential staff to come to work during certain categories of typhoon or rainstorm warnings. Both progovernment and pandemocratic unions called for a review of protections for workers during inclement weather, including legal protections.

Data on the number of labor inspectors working for the Department of Labor during the year were unavailable. Penalties for violations of minimum wage or occupational safety and health violations included fines, payments of damages, and worker's compensation payments. These penalties were sufficient to deter violations. The Occupational Safety and Health Branch of the Labor Department is responsible for safety and health promotion, enforcement of safety management legislation, and policy formulation and implementation; it enforced occupational safety and health laws effectively.

Employers and employer associations often set wages. Additionally, some activists claimed that employers used employment contracts that defined workers as "self-employed" to avoid employer-provided benefits, such as paid leave, sick leave, medical insurance, workers' compensation, or Mandatory Provident Fund payments. According to the Labor Department, there were cases in which employers faced heavy court fines for such behavior. The department held that it was seeking to promote public awareness, consultation, conciliation services, and tougher enforcement to safeguard employees' rights.

According to the General Household Survey conducted by the Census and Statistics Department during last year, approximately 17 percent of employees worked 60 hours or more per week. In the first quarter of last year, the Labor Department recorded 7,786 occupational injuries, including 2,404 classified as industrial accidents, most of which occurred in the construction, manufacturing, and transportation sectors. In the same period, there were five fatal industrial accidents. Employers are required to report any injuries sustained by their employees in work-related accidents. Labor activists continued to raise concerns about fatal industrial accidents, which primarily occurred in construction and infrastructure industries.

MACAU 2016 HUMAN RIGHTS REPORT

EXECUTIVE SUMMARY

Macau is a Special Administrative Region (SAR) of the People's Republic of China (PRC) and enjoys a high degree of autonomy, except in defense and foreign affairs, under the SAR's constitution (the Basic Law). A 400-member Election Committee reelected Chief Executive, Fernando Chui Sai-On, in 2014.

Civilian authorities maintained effective control over the security forces.

Prominent human rights problems reported during the year were limits on citizens' ability to change their government, constraints on press and academic freedom, and concerns regarding extradition of criminals to jurisdictions with harsher criminal punishments.

Trafficking in persons remained a problem, although authorities were building capacity to pursue trafficking cases. While there were continuing concerns that national security legislation passed in accordance with article 23 of the Basic Law in 2009 could compromise various civil liberties, from July 2015-June, the Macao SAR Government filed no cases against individuals or organizations in relation to this article.

The government took steps to prosecute and punish officials who committed abuses.

Section 1. Respect for the Integrity of the Person, Including Freedom from:

a. Arbitrary or Unlawful Deprivation of Life

There were no reports the government or its agents committed arbitrary or unlawful killings.

b. Disappearance

There were no reports of politically motivated disappearances.

c. Torture and Other Cruel, Inhuman, or Degrading Treatment or Punishment

The law prohibits such practices, and there were no reports government officials employed them.

Prison and Detention Center Conditions

Prison and detention center conditions generally met international standards, and the government permitted monitoring visits by independent human rights observers.

Physical Conditions: The Macau Prison, the SAR's only prison, has a maximum capacity of 1,565 persons, and the occupancy rate as of June was approximately 84 percent of capacity. As of June there were 1,317 inmates who were 16 years old (the age of criminal responsibility) and older; of these 1,116 were men and 201 were women. Offenders between the ages of 12 and 16 years old were subject to an "education regime" that, depending on the offense, could include incarceration. Between July 2015 and June, authorities held 16 juveniles at the Youth Correctional Institution, 15 male and one female.

Administration: The government's recordkeeping procedures were adequate. The government continued to use alternative sentencing for nonviolent offenders. Ombudsmen were able to serve prisoners and detainees. Authorities allowed prisoners and detainees reasonable access to visitors. Inmates are eligible for a weekly one-hour visit, with video visits arranged when necessary. Inmates with children may apply for weekend visits in a designated family room. Authorities permitted religious observance, including organized activities held within the prison. The law allows prisoners and detainees to submit complaints to judicial authorities without censorship and to request investigation of alleged deficiencies, and judges and prosecutors made monthly visits to prisons to hear prisoner complaints.

Independent Monitoring: According to the government, no independent human rights observers requested or made any visit to the Macau Prison. Judges and prosecutors visited the prison at least monthly.

d. Arbitrary Arrest or Detention

The law prohibits arbitrary arrest and detention, and the government generally observed these prohibitions. Activists expressed concern that the Macau Government abused prosecutorial procedures to target political dissidents, while police said they charged those they arrested with violations of the law.

Role of the Police and Security Apparatus

Civilian authorities maintained effective control over the Public Security Police (general law enforcement) and the Judiciary Police (criminal investigations), and the government had effective mechanisms to investigate and punish official abuse and corruption. There were no reports of impunity involving the security forces.

Arrest Procedures and Treatment of Detainees

Authorities detained persons openly with warrants issued by a duly authorized official based on sufficient evidence. Detainees had access to a lawyer of their choice or, if indigent, to one provided by the government. Detainees had prompt access to family members. Police must present persons in custody to an examining judge within 48 hours of detention. Detainees were promptly informed of charges against them. The examining judge, who conducts a pretrial inquiry in criminal cases, has wide powers to collect evidence, order or dismiss indictments, and determine whether to release detained persons. According to the government, courts should try defendants within the "shortest period of time." Investigations by the prosecuting attorney should end with charges or dismissal within eight months, or six months when the defendant is in detention. The pretrial inquiry stage must conclude within four months, or two months if the defendant is detained. By law the maximum limits for pretrial detention range from six months to three years, depending on the charges and progress of the judicial process; there were no reported cases of lengthy pretrial detentions. There is a functioning bail system; however, judges often refused bail in cases where sentences could exceed three years.

From June 2015-July, there were five complaints of police mistreatment reported to the Commission for Disciplinary Control of the Security Forces and Services of the Macao SAR and two complaints lodged with the Commission Against Corruption. All complaints were dismissed for lack of evidence. Authorities reported there was one case of death while in police custody during the second half of 2015. According to police the case concerned a Filipino man who was brought to a police station after illegally consuming narcotic drugs and psychotropic substances. Police said during their investigation, the man reported feeling ill, and police accompanied him to Conde S. Januario Hospital for treatment where he died of suspected myocardial infarction despite efforts to resuscitate him.

e. Denial of Fair Public Trial

The law provides for an independent judiciary, and the government generally respected judicial independence.

Macau's unique, civil-code law judicial system, which is derived from the judicial framework of the Portuguese legal system, operates within the PRC. The courts may rule on matters that are the responsibility of the PRC government or concern the relationship between central authorities and the SAR, but before making their final judgment, which is not subject to appeal, the courts must seek an interpretation of the relevant provisions from the National People's Congress Standing Committee (NPCSC). Macau's Basic Law requires that courts follow the NPCSC's interpretations when cases intersect with central government jurisdiction, although judgments previously rendered are not affected, and when the Standing Committee makes an interpretation of the provisions concerned, the courts, in applying those provisions, "shall follow the interpretation of the Standing Committee." As the final interpreter of the Basic Law, the NPCSC also has the power to initiate interpretations of the Basic Law.

Trial Procedures

The law provides for the right to a fair public trial, and an independent judiciary generally enforced this right. A case may be presided over by one judge or a group of judges, depending on the type of crime and the maximum penalty involved.

Under the law defendants enjoy a presumption of innocence, have access to government-held evidence relevant to their cases, and have a right to appeal. The law provides that trials be public except when the court rules otherwise to "safeguard the dignity of persons, public morality, or to provide for the normal functioning of the court." Defendants have the right to be informed promptly and in detail of the charges (with free interpretation), be present at their trials, confront witnesses, have adequate time to prepare a defense, not be compelled to testify or confess guilt, and consult with an attorney in a timely manner. The government provides public attorneys for those financially incapable of engaging lawyers or paying expenses of proceedings. The law extends these rights to all residents.

The judiciary provided citizens with a fair and efficient judicial process. Under the provisions of the civil procedural law, courts schedule hearings in civil cases after a series of procedural acts have been met to provide for the parties' rights at different stages of the judicial process. According to the government, as of June 30, the longest average waiting time for civil cases to be heard by a collegial panel of the Court of First Instance was 86 working days, while the average waiting time for cases to be heard officially by a sole judge was 29 working days. The average waiting time for criminal cases was less than one year, 84 working days involving someone on remand, and 210 working days in cases without remand. The average waiting time for cases to be heard by a sole judge was 56 working days. Activists said a lack of administrative capacity delayed the adjudication of both civil and criminal cases during the year.

Political Prisoners and Detainees

There were no reports of political prisoners or detainees.

Civil Judicial Procedures and Remedies

There is an independent and impartial judiciary for civil matters, and citizens have access to a court to bring lawsuits seeking damages for, or cessation of, a human rights violation. Due to an overloaded court system, a period of up to a year often passed between the filing of a civil case and its scheduled hearing.

f. Arbitrary or Unlawful Interference with Privacy, Family, Home, or Correspondence

The law prohibits such actions, and the government generally respected these prohibitions. The Office for Personal Data Protection acknowledged a continuing increase in complaints and inquiries regarding data protection.

Activists critical of the government reported the government monitored their telephone conversations and internet usage.

Section 2. Respect for Civil Liberties, Including:

a. Freedom of Speech and Expression

The law provides for freedom of speech and expression, and the government generally respected these rights.

The law criminalizes treason, secession, subversion of the PRC government, and theft of "state secrets," as well as "acts in preparation" to commit these offenses. The crimes of treason, secession, and subversion specifically require the use of violence, and the government stated it would not use the law to infringe on peaceful political activism or media freedom.

The Macau Penal Code states that anyone who initiates or organizes, or develops propaganda that incites or encourages, discrimination, hatred, or racial violence, will be liable to imprisonment for one to eight years. The law also states that anyone who, in a public meeting or in writing intended for dissemination by any means or media, causes acts of violence against a person, or group of persons on the grounds of their race, color, or ethnic origin, or defames, or insults a person, or group of persons on those grounds with the intention of inciting or encouraging racial discrimination, will be liable to imprisonment for between six months and five years.

During the year there were no arrests or convictions under this article.

<u>Press and Media Freedoms</u>: Independent media were active and expressed a wide range of views, and international media operated freely. The government heavily subsidized major newspapers, which tended to follow closely the PRC government's policy on sensitive political issues, such as Taiwan; however, they generally reported freely on the SAR, including criticism of the SAR government. Two independent media websites known to be critical of the Macau government alleged cyberattacks and intrusions prior to PRC Premier Li Keqiang's October visit to the Macau SAR.

<u>Violence and Harassment</u>: Activists alleged that authorities misused criminal proceedings to target government critics. There were no significant instances of violence or harassment directed at journalists.

<u>Censorship or Content Restrictions</u>: Activists raised concerns of media self-censorship, particularly because news outlets and journalists worried certain types of coverage critical of the government might limit government funding. Activists also reported the government had co-opted senior media managers to serve in various consultative committees, which also resulted in self-censorship. Journalists expressed concern the government's limitation on news releases about its own activities and its publishing of legal notices only in preferred media outlets influenced editorial content.

Internet Freedom

The government did not restrict or disrupt access to the internet or censor online content, and there were no reports the government monitored private online communications without appropriate legal authority.

According to the Statistics and Census Service, as of July there were 317,981 internet subscribers of a population of 646,800. This total did not take into account multiple internet users for one subscription, nor did it include those who accessed the internet through mobile devices.

The law criminalizes a range of cybercrimes and empowers police, with a court warrant, to order internet service providers to retain and provide authorities with a range of data. Some legislators expressed concern the law granted police authority to take these actions without a court order under some circumstances.

Twitter, which the PRC banned on the mainland, was available on the government-provided free Wi-Fi service. Activists reported they freely used Facebook and Twitter to communicate. Activists also reported the government had installed enterprise-grade software capable of censoring, decrypting, and scanning secured transmissions on its free Wi-Fi service without notifying users.

Academic Freedom and Cultural Events

Academics reported self-censorship and also reported that they were deterred from studying or speaking on controversial topics concerning China. Scholars also reported that they were warned not to speak at politically sensitive events or on behalf of certain political organizations. University professors reported the SAR's universities lacked a tenure system, which left professors vulnerable to dismissal for political reasons.

b. Freedom of Peaceful Assembly and Association

Freedom of Assembly

The law provides for freedom of assembly, and the government generally respected this right. The law requires prior notification, but not approval, of demonstrations involving public roads, public places, or places open to the public. In cases where authorities tried to restrict access to public venues for demonstrations or other public events, the courts generally ruled in favor of the applicants. Police may redirect demonstration marching routes, but organizers have the right to challenge such decisions in court.

Activists alleged authorities were making a concerted effort to use both intimidation and criminal proceedings against participants in peaceful demonstrations to discourage their involvement. Activists reported police routinely attempted to intimidate demonstrators by ostentatiously taking videos of them and advising bystanders not to participate in protests. Activists also stated authorities gave orders to demonstrators verbally rather than through written communication, which made it difficult to challenge their decisions in court. Activists reported the use of internal circulars and "rumors" threatening civil servants not to join politically sensitive events and demonstrations.

Further, activists alleged the Macau High Court had begun to adjudicate against defendants in freedom of assembly cases. In March, Macau police shrank the area requested by an antigovernment political organization to host an assembly in the Senado Square. The court upheld the restriction and dismissed the applicant's citation of law that "any restriction on the exercise of the right of peaceful assembly must conform to the strict tests of necessity and proportionality." In June approximately 400 persons participated in a vigil at Senado Square to mark the 27th anniversary of the 1989 Tiananmen Square crackdown.

Freedom of Association

The law provides for freedom of association, and the government generally respected it. No authorization is required to form an association, and the only restrictions on forming an organization are that it not promote racial discrimination, violence, crime, or disruption of public order, or be military or paramilitary in nature. The SAR registered 570 new organizations from July 2015 to June.

c. Freedom of Religion

See the Department of State's *International Religious Freedom Report* at www.state.gov/religiousfreedomreport/.

d. Freedom of Movement, Internally Displaced Persons, Protection of Refugees, and Stateless Persons

The law provides for freedom of internal movement, foreign travel, emigration, and repatriation and the government generally respected these rights. The Immigration Department cooperated with the Office of the UN High

Commissioner for Refugees (UNHCR) and other humanitarian organizations in providing protection and assistance to internally displaced persons, refugees, returning refugees, asylum seekers, stateless persons, and other persons of concern.

The Internal Security Law grants police the authority to deport or deny entry to nonresidents whom they regard under the law as unwelcome, as a threat to internal security and stability, or as possibly implicated in transnational crimes.

Protection of Refugees

<u>Access to Asylum</u>: The law provides for the granting of asylum or refugee status under the UN Convention Against Torture, and the government has established a system for providing protection to refugees. Persons granted refugee status ultimately enjoy the same rights as other SAR residents. The head of the SAR's Refugee Commission made clear that resource shortages and other priorities meant resolution of the cases would likely take several years.

Pending final decisions on their asylum claims, the government registered asylum seekers and provided protection against their expulsion or return to their countries of origin. Persons with pending applications were eligible to receive government support, including basic needs such as housing, medical care, and education for children.

Section 3. Freedom to Participate in the Political Process

The law limits citizens' ability to change their government through free and fair periodic elections, and citizens did not have universal suffrage. Only a small fraction of citizens played a role in the selection of the Chief Executive, who was chosen in August 2014 by a 400-member Election Committee consisting of 344 members elected from four broad societal sectors (which themselves have a limited franchise) and 56 members chosen from among the SAR's legislators and representatives to the National People's Congress and Chinese People's Political Consultative Conference.

Elections and Political Participation

<u>Recent Elections</u>: In 2014 a 400-member selection committee reelected Chief Executive Fernando Chui Sai-On. Chui ran unopposed and won 97 percent of the vote. The most recent general election for the 14 directly elected seats in the 33-member Legislative Assembly occurred in 2013. A total of 145 candidates on 20

electoral lists competed for the seats. The election for these seats was generally free and fair.

There are limits on the types of bills legislators may introduce. The law stipulates that legislators may not initiate legislation related to public expenditure, the SAR's political structure, or the operation of the government. Proposed legislation related to government policies must receive the chief executive's written approval before it is introduced. The Legislative Assembly also has no power of confirmation over executive or judicial appointments.

A 10-member Executive Council functions as an unofficial cabinet, approving draft legislation before it is presented in the Legislative Assembly. The Basic Law stipulates that the chief executive appoint members of the Executive Council from among the principal officials of the executive authorities, members of the legislature, and public figures.

Political Parties and Political Participation: The SAR has no laws on political parties. Politically active groups registered as societies or limited liability companies were active in promoting their political agendas. Those critical of the government generally did not face restrictions. Such groups participated in protests over government policies or proposed legislation without restriction.

Participation of Women and Minorities: There were no laws or practices preventing women or members of minorities from voting, running for office, serving as election monitors, or otherwise participating in political life on the same basis as men or nonminority citizens, and women and minorities did so. According to the Public Administration and Civil Service Bureau, as of June, there were 12,619 women working for the Macao SAR Government, 389 at the judicial organs and 60 at the Legislative Assembly. Women also held a number of senior positions throughout the government, including the secretary for justice and administration, the second-highest official in the SAR government. The Public Administration and Civil Service Bureau stated women were 43 percent of the SAR government, 56 percent of the judiciary, and 48 percent of the senior staff of the Legislative Assembly. One Executive Council member was from an ethnic minority, as was the police commissioner general. As of June, 38 female judges worked in the judiciary.

Section 4. Corruption and Lack of Transparency in Government

The law provides criminal penalties for official corruption, and there were few reported cases of officials engaging in corrupt acts.

Corruption: The government's Commission Against Corruption (CAC) investigated the public and private sectors and had the power to arrest and detain suspects. The Ombudsman Bureau within the CAC reviewed complaints of mismanagement or abuse by the CAC. There was also an independent committee outside the CAC entitled the Monitoring Committee on Discipline of CAC Personnel, which accepted and reviewed complaints about CAC personnel. According to Macau government statistics, in the second half of 2015 there were two complaints lodged at the CAC; however, no illegality was found. No complaints were lodged in the first half of the year.

Financial Disclosure: By law the chief executive, cabinet, judges, members of the Legislative Assembly and Executive Council, and executive agency directors must disclose their financial interests upon appointment, promotion, retirement, and at five-year intervals while in the same position. The information is available to the public on the website of the Macau Courts. The law states that if the information contained in the declaration is intentionally incorrect, the declarant shall be liable to imprisonment not exceeding three years or a fine, the amount of which shall not be less than 6 months of the remuneration of the position held. Additionally the declarant may be prohibited from being appointed to public office or performing public duties for up to 10 years.

Public Access to Information: The law does not provide for public access to government information. Nevertheless, the executive branch published online, in both Portuguese and Chinese, extensive information on laws, regulations, ordinances, government policies and procedures, and biographies of principal government officials. The government also issued a daily press release on topics of public concern. The information provided by the legislature was less extensive.

Section 5. Governmental Attitude Regarding International and Nongovernmental Investigation of Alleged Violations of Human Rights

Domestic and international groups monitoring human rights generally operated without government restriction, investigating and publishing their findings on human rights cases. Government officials often were cooperative and responsive to their views.

Section 6. Discrimination, Societal Abuses, and Trafficking in Persons

Women

<u>Rape and Domestic Violence</u>: The law criminalizes rape, including spousal rape, and the government effectively enforced the law. From July 2015-June, police received 25 complaints of rape and made 17 arrests.

In May, Macau's Legislative Assembly adopted the Law on Preventing and Combating Domestic Violence, but same-sex couples are not under its purview. Under the new law, a victim can decide whether to pursue charges if the consequences of the violence are "mild." The new law provides avenues for victims of domestic violence to leave dangerous environments as soon as possible and provides them with social services. Under the new law, the Social Welfare Bureau (SWB) is responsible for coordinating the application of protective and assistance measures to victims, such as temporary shelters, access to legal aid, financial assistance, health care, individual and family counseling, and assistance in access to education or employment. The law stipulates that a judge may order urgent coercive measures imposed upon the defendant individually or cumulatively, which can include: removing the offender from the victim's family residence; forbidding the offender to contact, harass, or pursue the victim; barring the offender from owning weapons, objects, or tools that can be used for perpetrating acts of domestic violence; or other measures aimed at preventing the reoccurrence of domestic violence. According to the government, the application of these measures does not preclude the possibility of prosecuting the perpetrators for criminal responsibilities as stipulated in the criminal code. From June 2015-July, police received 322 reports of domestic violence. Various NGOs and government officials considered domestic violence against women to be a growing problem.

The government made referrals for victims to receive medical treatment, and medical social workers counseled victims and informed them of social welfare services. During the first half of the year, the SWB handled 90 domestic violence cases. The government funded NGOs to provide victim support services, including medical services, family counseling, and housing, until their complaints were resolved. The government also supported two 24-hour hotlines, one for counseling and the other for reporting domestic violence cases.

NGOs and religious groups sponsored programs for victims of domestic violence, and the government supported and helped fund these organizations and programs. The Bureau for Family Action, a government organization subordinate to the

Department of Family and Community of the SWB, helped female victims of domestic violence by providing a safe place for them and their children and by providing advice regarding legal actions against perpetrators. A range of counseling services was available to persons who requested them at social service centers. Two government-supported religious programs also offered rehabilitation programs for female victims of violence.

Sexual Harassment: There is no law specifically addressing sexual harassment, unless it involves the use of a position of authority to coerce the performance of physical acts. Harassment in general is prohibited under laws governing equal opportunity, employment and labor rights, and labor relations. From July 2015-June, authorities received 13 complaints of sexual coercion and made 13 arrests.

Reproductive Rights: Couples and individuals have the right to decide the number, spacing, and timing of their children and the right to both fertility and contraceptive treatment, free from discrimination, coercion, and violence. Access to information on family planning, contraception, and prenatal care was widely available, as was skilled attendance at delivery and postpartum care.

Discrimination: Equal opportunity legislation mandates that women receive equal pay for equal work. Discrimination in hiring practices based on gender or physical ability is prohibited by law, and penalties exist for employers who violate these guidelines. The law allows for civil suits, but few women took cases to the Labor Affairs Bureau (LAB) or other entities. Gender differences in occupation existed, with women concentrated in lower-paid sectors and lower-level jobs. Observers estimated there was a significant difference in salaries between men and women, particularly in unskilled jobs. The CAC received no complaints of gender discrimination during the first six months of the year.

Children

Birth Registration: According to the Basic Law, children of Chinese national residents of Macau who were born in or outside the SAR and children born to non-Chinese national permanent residents inside the SAR are regarded as permanent residents. There is no differentiation between these categories in terms of access to registration of birth. Most births were registered immediately.

Child Abuse: Four cases of child abuse were reported to the authorities from June 2015-July. The SAR's Health Bureau handled 15 suspected child abuse cases during the year, all of which were transferred to appropriate governmental or nongovernmental institutions for follow up after hospitalization. In addition to providing measures to combat abuse, neglect, and violence against children by criminal law, the law establishes relief measures for children at risk. In this regard the SWB reported it handled 27 cases of abuse or neglect during the year.

<u>Early and Forced Marriage</u>: The minimum age of marriage is 16 years old. Children between ages 16 and 18 years old who wish to marry must get approval from their parents or guardians.

<u>Sexual Exploitation of Children</u>: The law specifically provides for criminal punishment for sexual abuse of children and students, statutory rape, and procurement involving minors. The criminal code sets 14 years as the age of sexual consent and 16 years old as the age for participation in the legal sex trade. The law prohibits child pornography. From July 2015-June, there were nine reported cases of child sexual abuse and five reported cases of rape of a minor. Police arrested seven suspects in reported cases of child sexual abuse and three suspects in cases of rape of a minor. Police received eight complaints and arrested seven in cases of sex with a minor during the same period.

<u>International Child Abductions</u>: The SAR is a party to the 1980 Hague Convention on the Civil Aspects of International Child Abduction. See the Department of State's *Annual Report on International Parental Child Abduction* at travel.state.gov/content/childabduction/en/legal/compliance.html.

Anti-Semitism

The Jewish population was extremely small. There were no reports of anti-Semitic acts.

Trafficking in Persons

See the Department of State's *Trafficking in Persons Report* at www.state.gov/j/tip/rls/tiprpt/.

Persons with Disabilities

The law prohibits discrimination against persons with physical, sensory, intellectual, and mental disabilities in employment, education, access to health care, or the provision of other state services, and the government generally enforced these provisions. The law mandates access to buildings, public facilities, information, and communications for persons with disabilities. The government enforced the law effectively. The government provides a variety of services to persons with disabilities, including discounted fares on wheelchair-accessible public transportation. The SWB was primarily responsible for coordinating and funding public assistance programs to persons with disabilities. There was a governmental commission to rehabilitate persons with disabilities, with part of the commission's scope of work addressing employment. There were no reports of children with disabilities encountering obstacles to attending school.

National/Racial/Ethnic Minorities

Although the government has made efforts to address the complaints of individuals of Portuguese descent and the Macanese (Macau's Eurasian minority), members of these two groups continued to claim that they were not treated equally by the Chinese majority.

Acts of Violence, Discrimination, and Other Abuses Based on Sexual Orientation and Gender Identity

There are no laws criminalizing sexual orientation or same-sex sexual contact and no prohibition against lesbian, gay, bisexual, transgender, or intersex (LGBTI) persons forming organizations or associations. There were no reports of violence against persons based on their sexual orientation or gender identity. LGBTI groups openly held several public events, and one registered LGBTI group openly lobbied the government and international organizations for an extension of protections to same-sex couples in a draft law on domestic violence.

HIV and AIDS Social Stigma

The law prohibits discrimination against persons with HIV/AIDS and limits the number of required disclosures of an individual's HIV status. Employees outside medical fields are not required to declare their status to employers. There were no reported incidents of violence or discrimination against persons with HIV/AIDS.

Section 7. Worker Rights

a. Freedom of Association and the Right to Collective Bargaining

The law provides workers the right to form and join unions or "labor associations" of their choice. The law does not provide that workers can collectively bargain, and, while workers have the right to strike, there is no specific protection in the law from retribution if workers exercise this right. The law prohibits antiunion discrimination, stating employees or job seekers shall not be prejudiced, deprived of any rights, or exempted from any duties based on their membership in an association. The law does not require reinstatement of workers dismissed for union activity.

Workers in certain professions, such as the security forces, are forbidden to form unions, take part in protests, or to strike. Such groups had organizations that provided welfare and other services to members and could speak to the government on behalf of members. Vulnerable groups of workers, including domestic workers and migrant workers, could freely associate and form and join unions, as could public servants.

In order to register as an official union, the government requires an organization to provide the names and personal information of its leadership structure. There is no law specifically defining the status and function of labor unions, nor are employers compelled to negotiate with them. The law provides that agreements between employers and workers shall be valid, but there is no specific statutory provision giving workers, resident or foreign, the right to collective bargaining. The government asserted striking employees are protected from retaliation by provisions of the law requiring an employer to have justified cause to dismiss an employee.

The government generally enforced the relevant legislation. The law imposes penalties ranging from MOP 20,000 to 50,000 ($2,500 to $6,300) for antiunion discrimination. Observers noted this may not be sufficient to deter discriminatory activity.

Workers who believed they were dismissed unlawfully could bring a case to court or lodge a complaint with the LAB or the CAC, which also has an Ombudsman Bureau to handle complaints over administrative violations. The bureau makes recommendations to the relevant government departments after its investigation.

Even in the absence of formal collective bargaining rights, companies often negotiated with unions, although the government regularly acted as an intermediary. There were no indications that disputes or appeals were subjected to lengthy delays. Pro-PRC unions traditionally have not attempted to engage in collective bargaining. The Macau Federation of Trade Unions acts as an adviser and assistant to those filing complaints to the LAB, which is responsible for adjudicating labor disputes.

b. Prohibition of Forced or Compulsory Labor

The law prohibits forced or compulsory labor. Penalties range from three to 12 years' imprisonment with the minimum and maximum sentences increased by one-third if the victim is under the age of 14 years old. Observers noted these penalties generally were considered sufficient to deter the use of forced labor. The government has a special, interagency unit to fight human trafficking, the Human Trafficking Deterrent Measures Concern Committee. In addition to holding seminars to raise awareness about human trafficking, the committee operates two 24-hour telephone hotlines, one for reporting trafficking and another to assist trafficking victims.

There were reports forced labor occurred in conjunction with commercial sexual exploitation of migrant women.

Also see the Department of State's *Trafficking in Persons Report* at www.state.gov/j/tip/rls/tiprpt/.

c. Prohibition of Child Labor and Minimum Age for Employment

A chief executive order prohibits minors under the age of 16 years old from working, although minors between ages 14 and 16 years old may work in "exceptional circumstances" if they obtain a health certificate to prove they have the "necessary robust physique to engage in a professional activity." Under the Labor Relations Law, "exceptional circumstances" are defined as: the minor (under the age of 16) has completed compulsory education and has the authorization of the Labor Affairs Bureau after hearing the Education and Youth Affairs Bureau's opinions; minors between 14 and 16 years of age may work for public or private entities during school summer holidays; minors of any age may be employed for cultural, artistic or advertising activities upon authorization of the Labor Affairs Bureau after hearing the Education and Youth Affairs Bureau's opinions and when such employment does not adversely affect their school attendance. Local laws do not establish specific regulations governing the number of hours children under 16 can work. The law governing the number of working hours (eight hours a day, 40 hours a week) was equally applicable to adults and legal working minors, but the law prohibits minors from working overtime hours. According to the civil code, minors 16 years old can acquire full legal capacity by emancipation if they get married, so they can deal with their personal matters and dispose their properties by themselves.

Minors below 16 years old are forbidden from certain types of work, including but not limited to domestic work, employment between 9:00 p.m. and 7:00 a.m., and employment at places where admission of minors is forbidden, such as casinos. The government requires employers to conduct an assessment of the nature, extent, and duration of risk exposure at work before recruiting or employing a minor. These regulations are intended to protect children from physically hazardous work, including exposure to dangerous chemicals, and jobs deemed inappropriate due to the child's age.

The LAB enforced the law through periodic and targeted inspections, and prosecuted violators. Regulations stipulate LAB inspectors shall be trained to look for child labor in order to carry out their responsibilities. Information on the penalties for violations was not available. Employers are obligated to provide professional training and working conditions appropriate to a minor's age to prevent situations that undermine his/her education and could endanger health, safety, and physical and mental development.

Child labor occurred, with some children reportedly working in family-operated or small businesses, while others were subject to commercial sexual exploitation (see section 6, Children).

d. Discrimination with Respect to Employment and Occupation

The Basic Law and the Labor Relations Law provides that all residents shall be equal before the law and shall be free from discrimination, irrespective of their nationality descent, race, sex, language, religion, political persuasion or ideological belief, educational level, economic status, or social conditions. The Labor Relations Law expands on this list to include discrimination based on national or social origin, descent, race, color, gender, sexual orientation, age, marital status, language, religion, political or ideological beliefs, membership of associations, education, or economic background (see section 6, Women). The law also states that all residents have a right to privacy as it relates to access to and disclosure of information related to their family life, emotional and sexual life, state of health, and their political and religious convictions. Local law requires employers to provide equal pay for equal work, regardless of gender. Between July 2015 and June, there were no cases of termination of employment due to HIV/AIDS infection.

There were no reports of the government failing to enforce the relevant laws but some discrimination occurred. For example, under the law migrant workers enjoy treatment equal to that of local workers, including the same rights, obligations, and remuneration. According to official statistics, at the end of July, there were 182,459 nonresident workers who accounted for approximately 28 percent of the population. They frequently complained of discrimination in the workplace. Most worked in the restaurant and hotel industry, but others are employed as domestic servants, in the hotel and hospitality industry, or in construction and retail trade.

e. Acceptable Conditions of Work

Local labor laws establish the general principle of fair wages and mandate compliance with wage agreements. Effective January 1, the mandatory minimum wage for security guards and cleaners was raised to MOP 30 ($3.75). The SAR does not calculate an official poverty line, and its median monthly income is MOP 13,000 ($1,625). The law provides for a 48-hour workweek (many businesses operated on a 40-hour workweek), an eight-hour workday, paid overtime, annual leave, and medical and maternity care. The law provides for a 24-hour rest period each week. The law does not define "temporary contract" or "short-term contract." It states only that a labor contract may be either for a defined term or of indefinite duration. All workers employed in the SAR, whether under a term contract or an indefinite contract, are entitled to such benefits as specified working hours, weekly leave, statutory holidays, annual leave, and sick leave. At the end of September, there were 10,822 part-time workers, accounting for 5.5 percent of total worker population. No data on the number temporary contract workers is available. The law does not apply to part-time workers and workers on temporary contracts.

The law includes a requirement that employers provide a safe working environment, and the LAB sets occupational safety and health standards. The law prohibits excessive overtime but permits legal overtime (up to eight hours, and irrespective of workers' consent) in force majeure cases or as a response to external shocks, at the discretion of the employer.

All workers, including migrants, have access to the courts in cases in which an employee is unlawfully dismissed, an employer fails to pay compensation, or a worker believes his/her legitimate interests were violated. Employers can dismiss staff "without just cause" if they provide economic compensation indexed to an employee's length of service.

The LAB provides assistance and legal advice to workers upon request, and cases of labor-related malpractices are referred to the LAB. From July 2015-June, the LAB provided assistance for 6,417 cases. Additionally, the LAB could charge the worker or union a fee to process such complaints.

The LAB enforced occupational safety and health regulations, and failure to correct infractions could lead to prosecution. There were approximately 140 labor inspectors in the country, which was adequate to enforce compliance; almost all inspectors held university degrees and most had more than five years' experience. Health Bureau guidelines protect pregnant workers and those with heart and lung diseases from exposure to secondhand smoke by exempting them from work in smoking areas, such as casinos.

Local employers favored unwritten labor contracts of indefinite duration, except in the case of migrant workers, who were issued written contracts for specified terms. Labor groups reported employers increasingly used temporary contracts to circumvent obligations to pay for worker benefits such as pensions, sick leave, and paid holidays. The short-term nature of written contracts made it easier to dismiss workers through nonrenewal. The law provides for workers to remove themselves from hazardous conditions without jeopardy to their employment, but some workers reported being dismissed for refusing to work in unhealthy environments.

The SAR recorded 7,499 workplace accidents from July 2015-June. Authorities recorded 17 workplace fatalities, of which seven were judged to have possible links to the individuals' preexisting health conditions. Most workplace injuries reported were minor, with one in seven injured workers returning to their duties the same day. Workplace injuries permanently incapacitated 22 persons.